SPIRITUAL
LEADERS AND
THINKERS

ELISABETH
SCHÜSSLER
FIORENZA

SPIRITUAL LEADERS AND THINKERS

JOHN CALVIN

DALAI LAMA (TENZIN GYATSO)

MARY BAKER EDDY

JONATHAN EDWARDS

DESIDERIUS ERASMUS

MOHANDAS GANDHI

AYATOLLAH RUHOLLAH KHOMEINI

MARTIN LUTHER

AIMEE SEMPLE McPHERSON

THOMAS MERTON

SRI SATYA SAI BABA

ELISABETH SCHÜSSLER FIORENZA

EMANUEL SWEDENBORG

SPIRITUAL
LEADERS AND
THINKERS

ELISABETH SCHÜSSLER FIORENZA

Glen Enander

Introductory Essay by
Martin E. Marty, Professor Emeritus
University of Chicago Divinity School

CHELSEA HOUSE
PUBLISHERS
A Haights Cross Communications Company
Philadelphia

COVER: Elisabeth Schüssler Fiorenza.

CHELSEA HOUSE PUBLISHERS

VP, NEW PRODUCT DEVELOPMENT Sally Cheney
DIRECTOR OF PRODUCTION Kim Shinners
CREATIVE MANAGER Takeshi Takahashi
MANUFACTURING MANAGER Diann Grasse

Staff for ELISABETH SCHÜSSLER FIORENZA

EXECUTIVE EDITOR Lee Marcott
EDITORIAL ASSISTANT Carla Greenberg
PRODUCTION EDITOR Noelle Nardone
PHOTO EDITOR Sarah Bloom
SERIES AND COVER DESIGNER Keith Trego
LAYOUT 21st Century Publishing and Communications, Inc.

A Haights Cross Communications ◤ Company

www.chelseahouse.com

First Printing

9 8 7 6 5 4 3 2 1

Library of Congress Cataloging-in-Publication Data

Enander, Glen.
    Elisabeth Schüssler Fiorenza / Glen Enander.
        p. cm.—(Spiritual leaders and thinkers)
    Includes bibliographical references and index.
        ISBN 0-7910-8105-2 (hardcover)
    1. Schüssler Fiorenza, Elisabeth, 1938– 2. Catholics—United States—
Biography. 3. Women theologians—United States—Biography. 4. Feminists—
United States—Biography. I. Title. II. Series.
BX4705.S51412E52 2005
230'.2'092—dc22
                                                            2004025646

All links and web addresses were checked and verified to be correct at the time
of publication. Because of the dynamic nature of the web, some addresses and
links may have changed since publication and may no longer be valid.

CONTENTS

Foreword

Why become acquainted with notable people when making efforts to understand the religions of the world?

Most of the faith communities number hundreds of millions of people. What can attention paid to one tell about more, if not most, to say nothing of *all*, their adherents? Here is why:

The people in this series are exemplars. If you permit me to take a little detour through medieval dictionaries, their role will become clear.

In medieval lexicons, the word *exemplum* regularly showed up with a peculiar definition. No one needs to know Latin to see that it relates to "example" and "exemplary." But back then, *exemplum* could mean something very special.

That "ex-" at the beginning of such words signals "taking out" or "cutting out" something or other. Think of to "excise" something, which is to snip it out. So, in the more interesting dictionaries, an *exemplum* was referred to as "a clearing in the woods," something cut out of the forests.

These religious figures are *exempla*, figurative clearings in the woods of life. These clearings and these people perform three functions:

First, they define. You can be lost in the darkness, walking under the leafy canopy, above the undergrowth, plotless in the pathless forest. Then you come to a clearing. It defines with a sharp line: there, the woods end; here, the open space begins.

Great religious figures are often stumblers in the dark woods.

We see them emerging in the bright light of the clearing, blinking, admitting that they had often been lost in the mysteries of existence, tangled up with the questions that plague us all, wandering without definition. Then they discover the clearing, and, having done so, they point our way to it. We then learn more of who we are and where we are. Then we can set our own direction.

Second, the *exemplum*, the clearing in the woods of life, makes possible a brighter vision. Great religious pioneers in every case experience illumination and then they reflect their light into the hearts and minds of others. In Buddhism, a key word is *enlightenment*. In the Bible, "the people who walked in darkness have seen a great light." They see it because their prophets or savior brought them to the sun in the clearing.

Finally, when you picture a clearing in the woods, an *exemplum*, you are likely to see it as a place of cultivation. Whether in the Black Forest of Germany, on the American frontier, or in the rain forests of Brazil, the clearing is the place where, with light and civilization, residents can cultivate, can produce culture. As an American moviegoer, my mind's eye remembers cinematic scenes of frontier days and places that pioneers hacked out of the woods. There, they removed stones, planted, built a cabin, made love and produced families, smoked their meat, hung out laundered clothes, and read books. All that can happen in clearings.

In the case of these religious figures, planting and cultivating and harvesting are tasks in which they set an example and then inspire or ask us to follow. Most of us would not have the faintest idea how to find or be found by God, to nurture the Holy Spirit, to create a philosophy of life without guidance. It is not likely that most of us would be satisfied with our search if we only consulted books of dogma or philosophy, though such may come to have their place in the clearing.

Philosopher Søren Kierkegaard properly pointed out that you cannot learn to swim by being suspended from the ceiling on a belt and reading a "How To" book on swimming. You learn because a parent or an instructor plunges you into water, supports you when necessary, teaches you breathing and motion, and then releases you to swim on your own.

Kierkegaard was not criticizing the use of books. I certainly have nothing against books. If I did, I would not be commending this series to you, as I am doing here. For guidance and courage in the spiritual quest, or—and this is by no means unimportant!—in intellectual pursuits, involving efforts to understand the paths others have taken, there seems to be no better way than to follow a fellow mortal, but a man or woman of genius, depth, and daring. We "see" them through books like these.

Exemplars come in very different styles and forms. They bring differing kinds of illumination, and then suggest or describe diverse patterns of action to those who join them. In the case of the present series, it is possible for someone to repudiate or disagree with *all* the religious leaders in this series. It is possible also to be nonreligious and antireligious and therefore to disregard the truth claims of all of them. It is more difficult, however, to ignore them. Atheists, agnostics, adherents, believers, and fanatics alike live in cultures that are different for the presence of these people. "Leaders and thinkers" they may be, but most of us do best to appraise their thought in the context of the lives they lead or have led.

If it is possible to reject them all, it is impossible to affirm everything that all of them were about. They disagree with each other, often in basic ways. Sometimes they develop their positions and ways of thinking by separating themselves from all the others. If they met each other, they would likely judge each other cruelly. Yet the lives of each and all of them make a contribution to the intellectual and spiritual quests of those who go in ways other than theirs. There are tens of thousands of religions in the world, and millions of faith communities. Every one of them has been shaped by founders and interpreters, agents of change and prophets of doom or promise. It may seem arbitrary to walk down a bookshelf and let a finger fall on one or another, almost accidentally. This series may certainly look arbitrary in this way. Why precisely the choice of these exemplars?

In some cases, it is clear that the publishers have chosen someone who has a constituency. Many of the world's 54 million Lutherans may be curious about where they got their name, who the man Martin Luther was. Others are members of a community but choose isolation: The hermit monk Thomas Merton is typical. Still others are exiled and achieve their work far from the clearing in which they grew up; here the Dalai Lama is representative. Quite a number of the selected leaders had been made unwelcome, or felt unwelcome in the clearings, in their own childhoods and youth. This reality has almost always been the case with women like Mary Baker Eddy or Aimee Semple McPherson. Some are extremely controversial: Ayatollah Ruhollah Khomeini stands out. Yet to read of this life and thought as one can in this series will be illuminating in much of the world of conflict today.

Reading of religious leaders can be a defensive act: Study the lives of certain ones among them and you can ward off spiritual—and sometimes even militant—assaults by people who follow them. Reading and learning can be a personally positive act: Most of these figures led lives that we can indeed call exemplary. Such lives can throw light on communities of people who are in no way tempted to follow them. I am not likely to be drawn to the hermit life, will not give up my allegiance to medical doctors, or be successfully nonviolent. Yet Thomas Merton reaches me and many non-Catholics in our communities; Mary Baker Eddy reminds others that there are more ways than one to approach healing; Mohandas Gandhi stings the conscience of people in cultures like ours where resorting to violence is too frequent, too easy.

Finally, reading these lives tells something about how history is made by imperfect beings. None of these subjects is a god, though some of them claimed that they had special access to the divine, or that they were like windows that provided for illumination to that which is eternal. Most of their stories began with inauspicious childhoods. Sometimes they were victimized, by parents or by leaders of religions from which they later broke.

Some of them were unpleasant and abrasive. They could be ungracious toward those who were near them and impatient with laggards. If their lives were symbolic clearings, places for light, many of them also knew clouds and shadows and the fall of night. How they met the challenges of life and led others to face them is central to the plot of all of them.

I have often used a rather unexciting concept to describe what I look for in books: *interestingness*. The authors of these books, one might say, had it easy, because the characters they treat are themselves so interesting. But the authors also had to be interesting and responsible. If, as they wrote, they would have dulled the personalities of their bright characters, that would have been a flaw as marring as if they had treated their subjects without combining fairness and criticism, affection and distance. To my eye, and I hope in yours, they take us to spiritual and intellectual clearings that are so needed in our dark times.

Martin E. Marty
The University of Chicago

1

A Childhood
Lesson Learned

*A fundamental methodological insight of historical
criticism of the Bible was the realization that the
Sitz im Lebem or life setting of a text is as important
for its understanding as its actual formulation.*

Elisabeth Schüssler Fiorenza, *In Memory of Her*

In the Eastern European country of Romania in September 1944, World War II is nearing its end, but battles are still being waged. As evening falls, a young girl and her family take refuge in an open field. They have fled their home to escape the dangers of the war. Now, each day, they find shelter wherever they can— perhaps in an abandoned barn or in a grove of trees. The little girl, Elisabeth, is only about six years old. She is cold and tired but she cannot sleep.

As young Elisabeth waits for sleep to come, she hopes for something small and simple that might bring her a little joy. She wants to receive a care package from America. She knows many other children have received packages from their relatives in the United States. Elisabeth, however, has no relatives in America. Too young to realize that no package will come, she waits and hopes. When nothing arrives, she feels left out, ignored, unimportant, and forgotten. Elisabeth will not forget the feeling of waiting and hoping for a care package that never seemed to come.

Decades later, when this little girl has transformed herself into one of the world's preeminent biblical scholars—known formally as Dr. Elisabeth Schüssler Fiorenza—the lessons of a childhood as a refugee would resonate in her writings. As a critical feminist biblical scholar, Schüssler Fiorenza has worked for decades to reshape the field of biblical studies. In so doing, she has taught, among other places, at two of America's most prestigious universities: Notre Dame and Harvard. Her success, however, did not come quickly or easily. She met with resistance, often from the very people and institutions she helped make notable through her groundbreaking work. Despite such opposition, Dr. Schüssler Fiorenza never compromised the lessons she learned as a child. Perhaps remembering the pain of feeling forgotten and left out, she continued to hope that "everyone would have enough to live, everyone would have their dignity, [and that] everyone would be able to do what they want to do."[1]

As Schüssler Fiorenza grew up, she became aware that some people had enough; some were simply guaranteed dignity; and some, because of their status, could generally do as they pleased. She also observed that the privileged people were generally men in positions of power, rather than women. Through her own experiences, her critical evaluation of society, and her interaction with oppressed people, she learned that what kept these people from having enough, from having dignity, and from having true freedom, was an assumption. That assumption was Western society's unspoken, yet very real idea that powerful men deserved to have power over less privileged men and women who supposedly had not yet earned their place among society's elite. Schüssler Fiorenza noticed that society assumed this power distribution was sensible, that it reflected the way things should be.

As a feminist biblical scholar, Schüssler Fiorenza also noticed a link between the methods used to interpret the Bible and the oppression of women and men who did not come from a privileged background. As her career in biblical studies progressed, Schüssler Fiorenza delved more deeply into this issue. She concluded that the Bible itself, and the interpretational practices used to explain it, quite often harmed rather than helped those who did not come from a privileged background.

She did not, however, abandon the Bible. Instead, she developed a multidimensional critique of the Bible and its interpretation. She not only criticized; she also created. As an alternative to traditional biblical interpretation, which is often harmful to those who do not come from a privileged background, she offered a multifaceted approach to biblical interpretation. Her approach was dynamic and complex, and took into consideration the consequences of biblical interpretation. Her method of interpretation contains within it the following ideas:

- It is incorrect to assume that one can achieve pure, ideologically neutral, or objective interpretation of the Bible. Interpretation is always done by humans, and humans always bring internal motivations and/or biases to their interpretations, especially when dealing with a socially influential text such as the Bible.

- For those people who do not come from a life of privilege, interpretations of the Bible tend either to uphold oppressive societal power structures or to resist such power structures in favor of fostering liberation for the masses.

- The means we use to evaluate different methods of biblical interpretation is less an issue of objectivity and more an issue of ethics. The question for Schüssler Fiorenza is this, "Does an interpretation tend to uphold or resist oppressive power structures?" If it upholds such structures, then the interpretation and/or the method of interpretation is inherently unethical.

Some claim that such reasoning is ideological (and therefore unrealistic). Schüssler Fiorenza responds by asserting that all ideas are, in some measure, ideological and the ideas and methods used in biblical interpretation are not immune. However, because the Bible so strongly influences society, choosing an ethical method of interpretation is of greatest importance. Perhaps the seeds of these seemingly complex ideas were planted when little Elisabeth felt the emotional pain of life as a refugee—feeling left out and forgotten.

Today, Elisabeth Schüssler Fiorenza's numerous books, magazine articles, and journal publications continue to challenge the established, traditional structure of biblical studies. Her effort to transform the discipline is two-fold. On one hand, she questions the very assumption upon which the field of biblical studies is based: that the goal of biblical studies is to find more and more objectively accurate facts within biblical texts. She argues that from the formation of the biblical texts to their translation and interpretation, there have been serious academic and societal problems. She points to a flaw she identifies as *kyriarchy*, a complex pattern of societal domination by elite males over those people who are not privileged.

On the other hand, Schüssler Fiorenza argues that it is not enough to solely point out the defects in the discipline of biblical studies; one must also propose an alternative theory. By her own example, she demonstrates that she believes scholars, and anyone else who interprets biblical texts, must work not only to correct flaws but also to create new definitions. They must work toward casting off the false assumptions of objectivity and neutrality in favor of recognizing an awareness of how biblical interpretations either help or harm people. In attempting this redefinition, Schüssler Fiorenza has had to overcome decades, even centuries, of traditional assumptions about biblical interpretations.

Elisabeth Schüssler Fiorenza hopes this newly defined field of biblical studies will include rather than exclude presently marginalized scholars and readers. She hopes it will inspire creative interpretation rather than insist on non-threatening repetition of societally safe ideas. For Schüssler Fiorenza, biblical studies should provide a "radical democratic space for discourse rather than perpetuate the present kyriarchal structure of conformity."[2] In other words, Schüssler Fiorenza hopes that her contribution to the field of biblical studies will increase the likelihood that no one, especially those who have been left out and excluded in the past, will ever have to feel excluded or silenced by the field of biblical studies again. On a wider scale, Schüssler Fiorenza wants to diminish the likelihood that anyone who waits for justice, true freedom, and a voice in society will feel the same hurt she felt as a young child waiting for a care package that never came.

In order to give voice to the voiceless and to remember those who were forgotten, Elisabeth Schüssler Fiorenza proposes an alternative to the traditional methods of biblical interpretation. She prefers a critical feminist hermeneutic of liberation as an ethical approach to biblical studies. In other words, she prefers a study of the methodological principles of interpretation of the Bible through the eyes of a critical feminist thinker. In order to better understand her ideas, we need to understand, among many others, three central terms she often uses to explain her methodology: *wo/man, conscientization,* and *kyriarchy.* Schüssler Fiorenza attempts to make people question their assumptions about the Bible and its interpretation. To do this, she often uses unfamiliar terms as a way to get people to think about the meaning of what they assume are familiar concepts.

Schüssler Fiorenza often uses the term *wo/man or wo/men* in order to call into her readers' consciousness the problematic nature of androcentric, or male-centered, language. Schüssler Fiorenza uses the word wo/men to refer to both women and men who experience oppression in any form. This term may appear in direct quotations in this book. Just as females have had to decide whether they are included in sentences such as "All men are created equal," or "One small step for man, one giant leap for mankind," Schüssler Fiorenza intends that both males and females will have to decide if the term wo/men applies to them when they read it.

For females and males to decide whether or not they are included in the term wo/men, they must become conscious of their social/power position, or lack thereof, in society. Determining whether one is an oppressed member of society is not, for Schüssler Fiorenza, an either/or question. One can oppress and be oppressed at the same time. Schüssler Fiorenza points out, however, that this position can, and often does, include multiple overlapping relationships. Becoming aware of how one is oppressed and is an oppressor is part of what Schüssler Fiorenza terms *conscientization*. It is a process that involves ridding oneself of years of seeing gender solely in terms of biology. Females and males must consider their gender as just one of several factors when they decide if they suffer under a kyriarchal structure of domination or oppression. For Schüssler Fiorenza, although females have throughout history been on the receiving end of an inordinate measure of human suffering, both females and males suffer when oppressive structures hurt them. Elisabeth Schüssler Fiorenza's feminism attempts to give a voice to all who are oppressed, regardless of their gender.

Schüssler Fiorenza invented the word *kyriarchy* herself because no other English word seemed adequate to express the concept. It comes from ancient Greek, from language in the New Testament, and fuses the Greek word for lord/master with the Greek word meaning "to rule or dominate." In contrast to patriarchy, which is generally construed as the power of all men over all women, kyriarchy denotes a socio-political structure in which elite men rule over both males and females. In other words, patriarchy has a biological concept of gender built into it, but kyriarchy refers to societally produced domination in which gender is only one factor among many others, such as social position and wealth. For Schüssler Fiorenza, while the male gender is generally privileged by society, both genders can be oppressed by elite males, depending on the circumstances.

For Elisabeth Schüssler Fiorenza the terms wo/men and kyriarchy are linked. She sees feminism as something that raises the consciousness of both females and males and helps them understand the oppressive structures that entangle them. Women and men, therefore, need first to understand their status when they are being oppressed, a difficult step since humans rarely like to feel oppressed. But they also need to understand their status as it relates to social, economic, political, and religious oppression, not only in terms of gender. Unfortunately, kyriarchal structures, as we will see in much greater detail later, work both to privilege elite men and to create the illusion that this situation of privilege is normal and should be considered nothing more than common sense. Indeed, traditional biblical interpretation assumes kyriarchy as a "God-ordained" system found in the pages of the Bible. Schüssler Fiorenza argues against this, and points out that women have suffered because of this line of reasoning. To understand that kyriarchal systems of oppression are not normal, healthy, or common sense is, for Schüssler Fiorenza, a major step toward liberation, and part of the process of conscientization.

That fact that women suffer under kyriarchal oppression, however, does not mean that they willingly admit to their situation or fully understand it. Because of this, Elisabeth Schüssler Fiorenza consistently argues for conscientization, the process of consciousness raising that allows women to understand and name the processes and structures of their oppression and the structures of privilege. This concept so infuses every aspect of Schüssler Fiorenza's writing that it might be said to shape her definition of a feminist biblical interpreter. This is partially why Schüssler Fiorenza argues for critical feminism. To critique one's situation, one must be conscious of it. Thus, people must become conscious of their oppression, and possibly how they participate, even unknowingly, in the oppression of others. Further, Schüssler Fiorenza argues that we all need to become conscious of the role that the Bible and its interpretation play in upholding or resisting kyriarchal structures of domination.

For Schüssler Fiorenza, both the field of biblical studies and the methods scholars, ministers, and laypeople use to interpret biblical texts are key centers of kyriarchy. Although some feminists see biblical studies as a field hopelessly mired in male-dominant thinking, Schüssler Fiorenza sees biblical studies as a field that cannot be abandoned into the hands of traditional interpreters.

She argues that too many people see biblical texts as central to their lives and spiritual journey to ignore the field. She proposes,

THE WOMEN'S LIBERATION MOVEMENT IN CHURCH AND ACADEMY

In addition to her childhood experiences as a refugee, the women's liberation movement also plays an integral part in Elisabeth Schüssler Fiorenza's life and in her biblical interpretations. In fact, she says "In my own experience, the existence of a wo/men's movement was critically important for articulating my theological self-identity in a new and different way." Speaking about the influence of the women's liberation movement in her life, Schüssler Fiorenza says ". . . only the wo/men's movement in society and church and its theoretical expressions in feminist and women's studies have enabled me to recognize that I articulate theology differently and conceptualize my discourse as a critical feminist theology of liberation." She has used this realization to continue to critically question not only the role of women, but also how theology and church leadership have traditionally been expressed.

Source: Ann Braude, ed., *Transforming the Faiths of Our Fathers* (New York: Palgrave Macmillan, 2004, pp. 138, 140).

therefore, among other remedies, the idea of a critical feminist biblical interpreter, one who can understand the structures of kyriarchy inherent both in the discipline of interpreting biblical texts and within the biblical texts themselves. She suggests that "becoming a feminist interpreter means shifting your focus from biblical interpretation construed as an ever better explanation of the text to biblical interpretation as a tool for becoming conscious of structures of domination and for understanding visions of a radical democracy that are inscribed in our own experience as well as in that of the texts."[3] This sentence, although somewhat complex, provides a suggestive summary of Elisabeth Schüssler Fiorenza's ideas. It implies a transformation *from* biblical interpretation that upholds the domination of women *to* a critical feminist biblical interpretation that resists it and seeks to liberate. Later we will discuss Schüssler Fiorenza's theory of biblical interpretation by dissecting this sentence. For now, we see that her method of biblical interpretation rests in a mind and heart transformed from acceptance of kyriocentrism to resistance of it within the context of biblical interpretation. Schüssler Fiorenza offers many suggestions to help her readers develop their ability to perform critical feminist biblical interpretation.

Elisabeth Schüssler Fiorenza has developed her methodology of critical feminist biblical interpretation over many years. To understand her method best, we need to consider one of the root metaphors she uses to explain her method and theory—dance. Schüssler Fiorenza sees the essence of what it means to be a critical feminist biblical interpreter in terms of dance. For example, to dance is to move, to express oneself, to make a gesture or turn, and then perhaps return to that same gesture or turn but in a slightly different way. Schüssler Fiorenza compares how one comes to understand her theories and feminist biblical interpretation in general to watching sunlight dancing in reflections on the ocean. In much the same way, the chapters of this book will dance, sometimes, as Schüssler Fiorenza might say, in spirals. We might introduce an idea, but realize that we need more context before we understand its particular movement within Schüssler Fiorenza's choreography. In other words, one should not be surprised to find that some ideas appear, disappear, and then appear again in a new form, just like the dance of light upon shimmering waters. It is also important to note that Schüssler Fiorenza's method of thinking is linear and logical, but also synthetic and creative. Her ideas intermesh with each other. Although we have gained a glimpse into the meaning of the terms wo/men, conscientization, and kyriarchy in this chapter, in later chapters we will see how these terms interrelate with other concepts. This will help to deepen our understanding of how they fit into Schüssler Fiorenza's dance of ideas.

We need to learn at least one more concept from Schüssler Fiorenza's metaphor of dance. Dancing is quite often performed to music. Sometimes the music is joyful and sometimes it is sorrowful. Sometimes, Schüssler Fiorenza warns, as women begin to learn the dance steps of the critical feminist hermeneutic of liberation and learn about the oppressive nature of traditional biblical interpretation, they feel as if the tone of the music they once loved has turned from joyous to sad. Schüssler Fiorenza assures her readers that this is not uncommon. Once women see that the pain caused by the oppression of kyriocentrism is often justified in the name of the Bible, a sense of loss occurs. What was once considered sacred must now be viewed with suspicion. This is, in a sense, a loss of innocence. For Schüssler Fiorenza, to become conscious of the structures of oppression is to move from a blind acceptance of traditional biblical religion to a new formation of it. Schüssler Fiorenza offers her readers more than a method of understanding the pain of oppression; she offers them the joy of *Wisdom-Sophia*.

Wisdom-Sophia is for Schüssler Fiorenza an alternative way of thinking about and personifying the divine. Within the male-centered system of biblical language it has generally been assumed that God is male: "God the Father" and "God the Son" are very common phrases. Because of the oppression of kyriocentric societies, however, this way of referring to the divine can often cause women to be oppressed. Schüssler Fiorenza suggests

BECOMING CONSCIOUS OF
ONE'S OWN SOCIAL SITUATION

One of Elisabeth Schüssler Fiorenza's central concepts, conscientization, means, at least in part, to gain an awareness of one's social status in comparison to others, and whether one suffers from structures of domination, participates in them, or both. To make it easier to understand the world's social structures, Carl Sagan imagined the world as a village and then researched what a village that reflected the world at large would look like. Schüssler Fiorenza might have asked some questions Carl Sagan did not ask, such as "How many women control how much of the wealth?" She would probably have joined with Sagan, however, in asking, "Where do you fit into the village?"

If we could shrink Earth's population to a village of precisely 100 people with all the existing human ratios remaining the same, it would look like this: There would be 57 Asians, 21 Europeans, 14 people from North and South America, and 8 Africans. Fifty-one people would be female; 49 would be male. Seventy people would not be white, while 30 would be white. Seventy people would not be Christian; 30 would be Christian. Fifty percent of the world's wealth would be in the hands of only six people, and all six people would be from the United States. Eighty people would live in substandard housing. Seventy people would be unable to read. Fifty people would suffer from malnutrition. One person would be near death; one would be near birth. Only one would have a college education. No one would own a computer. When one considers our world from such an incredibly compressed perspective, the need for both tolerance and understanding becomes apparent.

If we imagine our species as a village of 100 families it would look like this: 65 families in our village would be illiterate, and 90 would not speak English. Seventy families would have no drinking water at home. Eighty families would have no members who have ever flown in an airplane. Seven families would own 60 percent of the land and consume 80 percent of all the available energy. They would have all the luxuries. Sixty families would be crowded on 10 percent of the land. Only one family would have a member with a university education. And the air quality, water quality, and the climate would all be getting worse. What is our common responsibility?

Source: Carl Sagan, *Billions and Billions - Thoughts on Life and Death at the Brink of the Millennium* (New York: Ballentine Books, 1997).

instead that women see the divine as Wisdom-Sophia, a concept found within the biblical text itself, but one that is often ignored by male biblical interpreters. She invites her readers to practice critical feminist biblical interpretation within Wisdom-Sophia's house. She describes Wisdom-Sophia's house as a house of joy and learning where each person, regardless of their societal rank or financial status, shares equally in the opportunities for spiritual growth and societal participation. It is a house where radical democracy can thrive. It is a house where women who have been oppressed can experience joy and dance with others seeking divine Wisdom-Sophia. Schüssler Fiorenza's theory, therefore, deconstructs traditional biblical interpretation and sets in its place a critical feminist hermeneutic of liberation which leads to Wisdom-Sophia and a community of others who seek her. In this community, Schüssler Fiorenza argues that women need to strive to be heard.

This theme, then, of finding ways to move from oppressive structures supported by traditional methods of biblical interpretation toward liberation fostered by new methods of interpretation, is perhaps the central theme of Elisabeth Schüssler Fiorenza's work. It is also the theme and story of this book, thanks to a little girl who waited in vain for a care package from America, and who later came to America herself. Her arrival began a revolution that has started to shift the ideals of biblical interpretation from the perpetuation of the status quo to the empowerment of the oppressed. In this sense, Elisabeth herself brought a care package to America.

2

From Refugee to Pioneer

*The characteristic elements of my work
have their roots in this experience of war,
displacement, migration, and xenophobia.*

Elisabeth Schüssler Fiorenza,
"Wartime as Formative," *The Christian Century*

N ear the end of World War II, weary American soldiers marched down the sometimes dusty, sometimes muddy roads of Europe. As they traveled across Europe, perhaps the refugee families they met along the way reminded them of their own families, especially their children. For these soldiers, the sight of refugee children inspired a variety of generous gestures. One of the most popular of these gestures occurred when the soldiers threw the children some candy.

Similar to the scramble for candy and treats when a piñata breaks, the children scrambled to claim the sweet, tasty prizes from the soldiers. One girl, however, was too reserved, too shy to join the commotion. Although the soldiers probably did not think about it, the way they distributed the candy to the children rewarded those with physical strength and an aggressive attitude. But it left out those either too weak or too shy to fight. Once again, little Elisabeth found herself left out, only this time she understood why. Indeed, because she understood the reason she was left out, she began, even at this early age, to develop the foundational ideas of her later theories of liberation and feminism.

In the last chapter we learned about conscientization, the process of becoming aware of the societal structures that oppress women and men. This chapter paints a picture of how Elisabeth Schüssler Fiorenza came to comprehend and better understand her own oppression. This understanding transformed Schüssler Fiorenza from a confused young refugee at the end of World War II to one of the world's leading biblical scholars and transformers of biblical studies. Her early life as a refugee, her later struggles and triumphs as a student in Germany, and the existence of the women's liberation movement provide the background colors for the picture of Schüssler Fiorenza's lifelong passions. The picture includes dark hues, such as the memories of the violence she witnessed at the end of World War II. It also includes bold, resilient streaks of light, reflective of Schüssler Fiorenza's insistence that she be allowed to earn an education worthy of her abilities. In the foreground we find bright, vibrant splashes of color that symbolize Schüssler Fiorenza's rise to prominence as a critical feminist biblical scholar at one of the world's most prestigious universities.

Yet, even these bright colors will have within them some somber shades reflecting the ongoing struggle for the well-being and dignity of all women. Although she has risen to great heights in her profession, Schüssler Fiorenza's writing clearly shows she has never forgotten the ignored and the oppressed members of society. Her insistence that her readers remember and think deeply about the plight of oppressed people is found in her interviews, her magazine articles, her journal publications, and her books. By considering a few stories from her childhood, we can detect the origins of this consistent and fervent concern for the oppressed and forgotten members of society.

Elisabeth Schüssler Fiorenza describes the influence of her childhood, especially the war, this way: "The characteristic elements of my work have their roots in this experience of war, displacement, migration and xenophobia."[4] Elisabeth lived through all these tragedies, but as a child her mind saw them from a unique point of view. Her childhood memories of the horrible effects of the war, on herself, her family, and other victims of the war shaped not only her theology, but evidently her tastes and personality as well. One story she tells explains her lifelong addiction to sweets.[5] It also symbolizes the profound influence that Schüssler Fiorenza's childhood experiences had on her construction of a critical feminist hermeneutic of liberation.

As refugees, Elisabeth and her family often had to move from place to place in order to avoid violence in the most dangerous war zones. In 1944, fearful for their safety and perhaps even their lives, she and her family loaded up her uncle's horse-drawn wagon and fled their home. While the adults walked, the children spent much of the trip riding in the wagon.

As they traveled, her family had to beg for food along the way. Some people gave them food, but others did not. It was a harsh, day-to-day existence. One day, a generous person gave Elisabeth's family a real treat—a big strudel cake. As usual, the adults allowed the children to eat first. Of course, the children loved their sweet treat. But then something odd happened that confused Elisabeth. It was something she would remember all her life. As the children ate the cake, the adults started to cry. As a child, she did not understand this. For her, the simple joy of a eating the sweet strudel cake was her main focus. Later she would come to understand that the adults cried, not because of the joy they saw on the faces of their children, but because they believed sincerely that the children would likely never taste such a treat again. Although Schüssler Fiorenza argues that she did not understand the grownups' tears, the incident clearly left a mark on her memory. Indeed, Schüssler Fiorenza notes that this incident probably imbued in her a strong desire for sweets. The memory of this experience also inspired her to work for a world free from sorrow and pain.

Her wartime experiences did more than give Schüssler Fiorenza a sweet tooth. They also planted in her a deep concern for oppressed and forgotten people. This concern later developed in to a critical feminist theology of liberation. She remembers that as refugees at the end of the war, the adults tried to shield the children from some of the harsher realities of their situation. She recalls that "my mother and grandmother were always careful to stress that the Russian soldiers or the people who had refused us food or shelter along the way did not know any better."[6] She describes the environment her mother and grandmother created for the children, even in the midst of homelessness, hunger, and war as one where she learned about her "human dignity and claim to justice"[7] The women in her family created around her a ring of safety and love.

The ideals her grandmother and mother taught her, however, must have seemed to Elisabeth to be in conflict with the realities of Europe during the war. As she grew up and became an adult, she pondered and lived out those ideals, but she also remembered and suffered from the harsh realities of her youth. Schüssler Fiorenza admits that she "dreamt for years about shootings and explosions with fire everywhere."[8] Despite this, she asserts that her situation could have been worse. In contrast to herself, she recounts that a friend of hers, a little girl about her age, had to live through a night when her city was bombed. Recalling her friend's reaction to this traumatic night, Schüssler Fiorenza remembers that her friend's "hair turned grey overnight."[9] Although young Elisabeth did not live an easy life as a refugee at the end of the war, she also noticed, remembered, and grew conscious of the pain, problems, and trauma of others.

In this sense, her childhood, and especially the way she later interpreted it, inspired her not to forget the forgotten; not to overlook their suffering; and not to demean, diminish, or disregard those who live under oppressive societal structures. Elisabeth Schüssler Fiorenza's childhood experiences during World War II helped her grow ever more conscious of the situation of women in kyriocentric societies. As we will learn later, her adult interpretation of her childhood experiences also helped to inform and shape her theories and ideals. Fortunately, when the war ended, Elisabeth's life became more settled. On the last night of the war she recalls listening to the sounds of the cows roaming about and her family snoring as they all slept together in a barn. She did not understand that the end of the war would forever change her life.

After the war, Elisabeth and her family moved to a rural village in Germany where her father became a tailor. Now, for the third time, because of her travels as a refugee, she would enter the first grade. Despite her turbulent early childhood during the war, Elisabeth did quite well in school. At one point during her grade school education, she did so well on her examinations that she qualified for the advanced track. Eventually, Elisabeth qualified for a university education, a high honor in the German education system of the day. Because she grew up Catholic in a rural area of Germany, Schüssler Fiorenza recounts that her academic success was a "statistical miracle."[10] In a largely Lutheran country

OFTEN FORGOTTEN:
REFUGEES IN THE MODERN WORLD

Elisabeth Schüssler Fiorenza's early childhood experiences as a refugee helped shape her life as an adult and a feminist and planted within her a concern for those in need that has grown and flourished over the years. Her refugee experience occurred near the end of World War II, the last "world war," but certainly not the last military conflict to produce significant refugee populations. From Southeast Asia to Africa, Europe, Latin America and elsewhere around the world, refugees have in the past fifty years been forced to flee their homes in fear for their lives. Although the number of refugees has declined over the past decade, the scope and intensity of the problem continues.

One common problem that refugees face is the fact that they are often mistrusted and undervalued. Potential host countries and communities often feel that they cannot afford to help. Refugees, however, frequently add much to the societies that grant them asylum. Albert Einstein, who came to the United States in 1933 to escape Nazi Germany, is a famous refugee who made many meaningful contributions to his new country. Other refugees, however, without fame or fortune, also contribute to the economies, cultures, and social well-being of the nations that take them in. As a refugee from Tibet, Tenzin Gyasto, recipient of the Nobel Peace Prize, has fostered an understanding of Buddhism and an awareness of nonviolent resistance since being forced to flee his home country.

According to experts, in addition to the difficult way of life that all refugees face, female refugees can also face distinct problems because of their gender. Social attitudes about what a female should and should not do can harm a female refugee's chances of obtaining employment in some host countries and communities. Because many refugees are females who have lost their husbands to war, social attitudes can severely hamper their efforts to build a new life. Still, female refugees have succeeded and continue to do so. For example, Golda Meir, a Jewish refugee whose family fled from Russia to Canada and eventually to the United States, became the world's third female prime minister when she became Prime Minister of Israel in 1969.

Source: Gil Loescher and Ann Dull Loescher, *The Global Refugee Crisis: A Reference Handbook* (Santa Barbara, Calif.: ABC-CLIO 1994).

that was moving more and more toward urbanization, a rural Catholic girl who was an outstanding success at school was, indeed, out of the ordinary.

Her sharp mind and active imagination were the main reasons for her academic success. She recalls that when she first "published" in third grade, she wrote that she would one day like to be Pope. Her youthful common sense and sharp mind saw no reason for a barrier of gender discrimination to keep her from any dream she wished to achieve. Later in her career, however, she mused, "I'm not too sure whether I still wish it."[11]

From an early age Elisabeth viewed the assumptions of her elders with marked suspicion. Wondering about the notion of the church as the "Father's" house, she once put on a dress as if it were Mardi Gras and painted her face. She then went to her local parish church when it was empty and stood inside laughing "loudly for many minutes."[12] She recalls that the "ground did not open and swallow her as . . . anticipated."[13] Perhaps this seems a bit comical, but for Elisabeth, it moved her to become suspicious of the church's teachings about God, as well as many other teachings the church claimed came from God. This suspicion would never leave her, and, when she became a professor, formed a major element in her critical feminist hermeneutic of liberation.

With an agile mind ready to question the authority of what she was taught, both religiously and academically, Elisabeth conquered her classes and emerged years later with a doctoral degree in theology. The journey to this accomplishment, however, did not occur without obstacles. Indeed, despite her suspicions of church teaching, her own youthful religious fervor might well have prevented her from reaching the pinnacle of success in the academic world. During Elisabeth's teenage years, she contemplated taking vows and becoming a nun. Her pastor, however, advised against it because he perceived she did not have a "vocation to obedience."[14] The advice proved wise.

THE EDUCATIONAL PATH:
FROM GERMANY TO AMERICA

The chronological summary of Elisabeth's years of studies indicates the rigorous academic/theological training she underwent. In 1958, she graduated from the gymnasium (the German version of college preparatory classes or prep schools in America). She then began studying German literature, history, and theology at the university level. Out of these fields, she chose theology as her course of study for her Master of Divinity degree, which she earned in 1962. In 1963, she received her licentiate, an academic degree ranking below that of a doctor given by some European universities. From 1964 to 1970 she worked toward and earned a doctorate in theology. Soon after that, she came to America to teach.

By any measure, her academic path through the German system of theological higher education is impressive. Her dissertation won the award for the best dissertation, as voted by the faculty of her university. When one considers, however, that Elisabeth spent most of her journey through the higher education system in Germany as the only female student in almost all of her classes, and the only female among many males taking her particular theological course of study, her accomplishments become even more impressive. Although some professors assisted her, others did not. Some, in fact, were plainly hostile to the idea of a female earning an advanced degree in theology. The story of how she earned that degree, with firm resolve, reflects her childhood willingness to challenge assumptions. It also shows her strong desire to fight against kyriocentrism for the well-being of women. In her academic battle, one can also detect the beginnings of several key elements of her critical feminist theory.

Examples of what she achieved as a university and graduate student abound. As mentioned earlier, her rural, Catholic background made her arrival at the college level anomalous. Once at the university, however, she could have chosen among a variety of academic paths. After a few years, she chose theology, which in Germany in 1960 was a field dominated by men. Nevertheless, she succeeded. Not only did she graduate with the equivalent of a master of divinity degree in 1962, but in 1964 she also had her licentiate thesis published as a book about pastoral theology with the specific focus on "ministries of women in the church."[15] Others informed her later that in its book form, her thesis could have earned her a doctorate. This seems credible because Elisabeth graduated *summa cum laude*—with highest distinction.

She started her doctoral studies at the University of Würzburg working with Rudolf Schnackenburg. Despite her impressive credentials, as the first female to take the full theological degree path, she felt out of place. She remembers a particular class session early in one semester when she had chosen to wear a red sweater to class. She recalls that the brightly colored sweater made her stand out from among the over one hundred other students—all men. When the professor entered the classroom he said, "Welcome lady and gentlemen."[16] The students were mostly seminarians who wore black. There were also some Franciscans among them—an order of monks devoted to preaching, missions, and charity—so they were wearing brown. When they turned to see the "lady" to whom the professor referred, Elisabeth's bright red sweater stood out in a sea of black sprinkled with brown. She recalls that she did not wear that red sweater to class again. Humorous as Schüssler Fiorenza finds the story, she also sees in it a symbol of the type of difficulty—social and kyriarchal, not academic—that she had as a woman completing her degrees in theology. After a short time at Würzburg, kyriarchal attitudes put another obstacle in her path.

Even with a master of divinity degree and licentiate in pastoral theology—and both degrees earned with highest honors—she recalls that although Schnackenburg had three fellowships to distribute, he told her bluntly that "I need to give them to those who have a future in theology, and as a woman you have no future in theology."[17] He also thought that laypeople could not teach theology at the university at that time. She admits that this "devastated" her.[18] She had done everything a graduate student could do, and she had done it quite well. She had graduated with highest honors. Still, this was not enough to overcome the kyriarchal attitude of her professor. He looked at her gender, not at her work and academic achievements.

Fortunately, she met another professor with whom she had worked, Josef Schreiner, from the University of Münster. He offered her a research position at his university. The move to Münster provided the opportunity for Elisabeth to meet Francis Fiorenza, the man that would later become her husband. She recalls that Francis "always jokes that we were lucky that I did not receive that scholarship, for otherwise we would never have met."[19] From 1964 to 1970, at Münster, Elisabeth flourished. Although at first she encountered difficulties finding enough like-minded readers to advise her on her dissertation, she eventually won the prize in 1970 for the best dissertation, a prize awarded at the discretion of the faculty of Münster.

Just as Elisabeth's childhood helped form her critical feminist theory, her path through the German higher educational system also shaped her. She characterizes the German system of higher education in theology, despite its kyriocentric bias, as a more academically inclusive system than the system she encountered when she arrived in America. She points out that, in the German system, the boundaries between "scientific exegesis and theology" were distinct, but were allowed to blend. To this day, she remains "shocked by the division to be found in [America] . . . between exegesis or historical criticism and theology."[20] As a critical feminist theorist of liberation, Schüssler Fiorenza today employs a variety of theoretical frameworks and often blends them together. The division-of-labor model in American theological higher education does not serve her well, and indeed her theories have served as a catalyst for serious debate on this issue.

During her academic career, her personal and educational interests centered on women and the kyriarchal structures in which they live, although she did not have the language to describe those interests at the time. Indeed, because she was already producing unique, original theoretical work, she recalls, I had to "provide the theoretical-theological framework for it myself."[21] During her journey through higher education, she wrote on topics that affected women, such as the ministry of women in the church, and the discernable presence of the grace of God in women who ministered in the church. She even argued that if seminarians, mostly men, were to learn to live and interact in the secular world, then women needed to be present in the seminaries. After all, women were quite a presence in the outside world. This was a shocking suggestion, given the prevailing attitudes in the 1960s in Germany. She remembers that even her advisor, who wrote the preface to the book in which she made this argument, was "nervous" about writing the preface, given the controversial nature of her argument.[22] The need, however, for Schüssler Fiorenza to construct theoretical frameworks even early in her academic career served her well. Later, in her teaching career in America, she presented the possibility of paradigm shifts—alternate perspectives—in biblical studies and hermeneutics.

Finally, just as when she was a refugee as a child, Schüssler Fiorenza felt like an outsider in the German theological higher educational system. Later in life, Schüssler Fiorenza would remember what it felt like to be the only female to take the full course in theology. She would remember what it felt like to be the only female in most of her classes. She would remember most of all what it felt like to be qualified for fellowships and scholarships, and yet to be refused for no other reason than because she was a woman. Because of this, Elisabeth Schüssler Fiorenza understood the problems, challenges, and structural biases inherent in higher educational settings in the 1960s. Throughout her teaching career in America, she never lost her awareness of this problem, and today still argues for a shift in these attitudes and a reformation of the kyriocentric structures of oppression that still exist in academic life. Her search for a theoretical framework from which to change kyriocentric paradigms would develop over the next thirty years.

THE NOTRE DAME YEARS

For Elisabeth Schüssler Fiorenza, the old cliché held true—although her formal education ended, she never stopped learning. She brought to America the wonder and curiosity of her childhood combined with the resilience and academic prowess of her theological education. After fourteen years at the University of Notre Dame, one of America's most prestigious Catholic universities, Schüssler Fiorenza eventually found her way to Harvard University, one of America's most admired schools. From a distance, one can read Schüssler Fiorenza's professorial career as a long and distinguished progression of successes. A closer inspection, however, reveals that similar to the trials she experienced in childhood and during her formal education, her years as a professor, especially at the University of Notre Dame, were less than idyllic, due largely to kyriarchal attitudes.

In the early 1970s, Elisabeth Schüssler Fiorenza began her American teaching career at Notre Dame. She was not the only woman in the theology program, as she had been at Warzburg, but in American academic circles she was certainly unique. At a meeting of the Society of Biblical Literature she discovered that she was the only married woman who enjoyed full-time employment in an academically theological position. At that time, academia generally assumed men would be the scholars and women would support them. Even though she held a professorship at an elite Catholic university, she would often be introduced as "wife and mother," instead of Dr. Schüssler Fiorenza, her academic title.[23] She argues that the roles of wife and mother were safe roles in society. They were the roles that the academic world valued in women over their intellectual or academic abilities.

Even so, Elisabeth Schüssler Fiorenza did not take the safe professional path. Soon after arriving in America, she volunteered and became co-chairperson of the American Academy of Religion/Society of Biblical Literature's Women's Caucus. Others warned her that getting involved in women's issues would harm her academic career. Nevertheless, Elisabeth Schüssler Fiorenza continued to involve herself in women's issues, both in her chosen discipline of biblical studies, and in the wider field of social criticism.

During the fourteen years after she came to America, Dr. Elisabeth Schüssler Fiorenza taught theology at the University of Notre Dame. Her early teaching years coincided with the height of the Vietnam War and a tone of general social upheaval in the United States. When Schüssler Fiorenza made a comment about the war during a class, two Notre Dame football players took offense. After class they suggested that Schüssler Fiorenza, because she was not an American citizen, should not criticize America. As an outsider—a female professor from Germany—teaching in an atmosphere in which explosive issues seemed to permeate the air, she recalls that she "struggled to survive."[24]

Her classes were attended only by males, and, because Notre Dame required four theology courses of all undergraduates at that time, were generally composed of students avoiding the war or students who were simply trying to fulfill a requirement. Few of her undergraduate students actually wanted to be in class. She recalls that the students in her first class "could not have cared less about what I had to teach about the Bible."[25] Despite this, Elisabeth Schüssler Fiorenza received from her students "the highest student ratings."[26] She taught both undergraduate and graduate classes, and remembers her graduate students were "wonderful."[27] Despite her status as an outsider, and despite warnings that her involvement in women's issues would harm her career, Schüssler Fiorenza continued to teach at the University of Notre Dame. Near the end of her time at Notre Dame, she wrote a book. Her book, *In Memory of Her: A Feminist Theological Reconstruction of Christian Origins*, would challenge the very paradigms of biblical studies upon which the discipline was built.

The title of Schüssler Fiorenza's book tells us a great deal about her philosophy. After the colon, Schüssler Fiorenza chooses the article "A" instead of "The" to begin the title. As a scholar, she never insists that one particular reading or interpretation of scripture should be inscribed as *the* definitive interpretation for all time. Further, in contrast to so-called "value-neutral" biblical interpreters, she proclaimed from the start that her book came from a feminist stance. While others hid their ideological presuppositions, Elisabeth Schüssler Fiorenza explained and defended hers. The next two words, "theological reconstruction" are technical. Theology means "the study of God." Reconstruction, of course, implies taking something that is in some way damaged, and putting it back together. According to Schüssler Fiorenza, the methods and content of biblical studies concerning Christian origins do indeed require reconstruction, mainly because in their present form they are generally harmful to women.

The phrase in *In Memory of Her* refers to the nameless woman that anointed Jesus' feet. About her act of devotion and love, the Gospel of Mark claims Jesus said, "And truly I say to you, wherever the gospel is preached in the whole world, what she has done will be told in memory of her"[28] Unfortunately, the specific name of this woman who anointed Jesus has been erased from memory by the male writers of the New Testament scriptures. Elisabeth Schüssler Fiorenza points out that although we do not know this woman's name, the gospel writers make a point of recording the name of Judas, man who betrayed Jesus, and Peter, another man who denied him. This story exemplifies the biases and androcentric tendencies inherent within biblical texts.

In Memory of Her jolted many scholars and members of the clergy from their comfortable interpretive assumptions. Schüssler Fiorenza's hermeneutical framework in *In Memory of Her* challenged the assumption that biblical texts fell out of the mouth of God onto the page. It also challenged the traditional academic assumption that scholars should divest themselves of ideological lenses when interpreting biblical texts. Dr. Elisabeth Schüssler Fiorenza angered both groups: biblical scholars because of her challenge to divine revelation, and value-neutral scholars because of her challenge to the very notion of the possibility that anyone, at anytime, can actually be value-neutral, especially when the text itself was replete with kyriocentrism and androcentric language.

On the other hand, the book received warm and enthusiastic welcome from women who finally had an example of a methodology they could use to expose and to resist the androcentric, kyriarchal nature of the biblical texts that had for so long been used to oppress them. In the introduction to the tenth anniversary edition of the book, Elisabeth Schüssler Fiorenza indicates that although many in the academic world complained about *In Memory of Her* because of its erudite tone, other women—less educated but perhaps more willing or eager to learn about Schüssler Fiorenza's theories—worked their way through the book with enthusiasm and joy. They found themselves empowered with a critical feminist hermeneutical method of interpretation with which to counter those who would oppress them and would use the Bible as an excuse to do it. To challenge, however, divine revelation on the one hand, and to undermine the core values of academia on the other, came at a price for Elisabeth Schüssler Fiorenza. Soon after *In Memory of Her* was published, Schüssler Fiorenza was made to feel even more like an outsider at Notre Dame, and eventually felt it necessary to leave.

Elisabeth Schüssler Fiorenza's break with the University of Notre Dame in 1984 was triggered by several issues. First, she encountered problems because she refused to be reduced to undergraduate teaching. Although she and her husband had written into their contracts the fact that they would have equal teaching positions in the graduate and undergraduate programs, there were attempts to restrict her to undergraduate teaching. At the time, a common stereotype existed that said that men did graduate teaching while women did undergraduate teaching. After Schüssler Fiorenza earned and Notre Dame granted her tenure in 1975, some at Notre Dame seemed to question whether or not she should even be at the school. Before Notre Dame granted Elisabeth Schüssler Fiorenza tenure, surely the university must have understood Schüssler Fiorenza's willingness and desire to engage in women's issues. For example, in 1971, she agreed to cochair the women's caucus of the Society of Biblical Literature with Carol Christ. Further, she also was a member of the New York Feminist Scholars in Religion and also a member of the American Academy of Religion Task Force on the Status of Women in the Academic Study of Religion. Thus, knowing Schüssler Fiorenza's stance as a critical feminist biblical scholar, in 1975, Notre Dame conferred tenure upon her. Unfortunately, the relationship between Dr. Schüssler Fiorenza and the University of Notre Dame was destined to end.

In addition Elisabeth Schüssler Fiorenza spoke at two Women's Ordination Conferences, in 1975 and 1978. The department chairperson was against women's ordination, and the university had received many protest letters from alumni and donors. The chairperson also objected to an article Schüssler Fiorenza published in 1975 (after she had received tenure) on "Feminist Theology as a Critical Theology of Liberation" and called her into his office three different times to object to her ideas. He also told her that someone with such ideas should not teach at Notre Dame. Schüssler Fiorenza indicated that "this started all my problems at Notre Dame."[29] She added, "I share this in order to point out that you cannot do feminist theology without ramifications. You have to pay the price."[30] Evidently Schüssler Fiorenza could be a critical feminist biblical scholar as long as she did not speak her mind in a public forum.

But she did speak, and continued to press for the well-being of women, and again, just as in her childhood, her years of college and graduate school, and her early years in America, Elisabeth Schüssler Fiorenza found herself, at least metaphorically, on the outside. She remembers Notre Dame and her problems there as a set of experiences that "helped me clarify my notion of feminist theology both as a critical and as a liberation theology of struggle."[31] Her struggles at the University of Notre Dame continued for almost a decade before she finally decided to leave.

At its core, Elisabeth Schüssler Fiorenza's theoretical investigations into and practical advocacy of a critical feminist hermeneutic of liberation created serious conflict. After the publication of *In Memory of Her*—widely acknowledged as a groundbreaking work in the field of biblical studies—Schüssler Fiorenza was not allowed to use her own book in her own classes at Notre Dame. For those unfamiliar with the academic world, the depth of this insult may not be immediately obvious. But consider that professors are hired not only for their ability to teach, but also for their academic ability to discover, propose, and publish new ideas. To disallow professors to use their published academic works is to argue that their work is so inferior that the university does not want to take the chance that it will harm the intellectual development of its students. By any objective standard, however, *In Memory of Her* meets and surpasses standards of academic excellence. The issue for the University of Notre Dame, and the chairman of the religion department, was the content of Schüssler Fiorenza's critical feminist hermeneutic of liberation. Schüssler Fiorenza recalls that when instructed not to use *In Memory of Her* in her classes, she was told to do "straight exegesis." In other words, Notre Dame's ideological stance concerning Elisabeth Schüssler Fiorenza argued that her ideology of liberation was at odds with their "neutral" stance, which *In Memory of Her* demonstrates is not neutral, but hostile to women. Of course, ironically, their "neutral" stance necessitated the ideological censorship of her most important and most respected work.

Censorship from the university at which she taught proved too much for Schüssler Fiorenza. After leaving Notre Dame, she taught at the Episcopal Divinity School in Cambridge, Massachusetts. In an interview conducted just after the move, she reflected that she had to leave Notre Dame because of the futility of trying to develop her theories in an institution set against their existence. From this experience, she began to develop her idea of the "church on the move."[32] She theorized that with Vatican II, "wo/men and not just the hierarchy are church." Much in keeping with her move to an Episcopal theological school, she suggested that women who felt the need to serve in a parish might do well to leave the Catholic Church in favor of serving where they would be accepted. Later, Schüssler Fiorenza would argue for a wholly reshaped and recreated church she would call the "*ekklēsia* of women," a dynamic alternative for women to the kyriarchal church system.

Elisabeth Schüssler Fiorenza's problems with Notre Dame may not have been wholly unique. She remembers the advice she received from a friend of hers, a Catholic professor, teaching at a Protestant college. He said, "Elisabeth, in the next twenty years or so, however long the Pope lives and the reaction lasts, nobody will be able to do Catholic theology with integrity in a Roman Catholic Institution."[33] Her troubles with the University of Notre Dame, however, proved transformational. They provided a catalyst for much of her later theory about kyriarchal structures of both the traditional church and the supposedly neutral world of academia.

FROM NOTRE DAME TO HARVARD

After leaving Notre Dame in 1984, Elisabeth Schüssler Fiorenza had more freedom to explore and develop her critical feminist hermeneutic of liberation. Her four years at the Episcopal Divinity School allowed her both to teach and to advocate for critical feminist biblical interpretation. She characterized the change as one that gave her the opportunity "for the next twenty years of my teaching life to teach women—and other students who are interested—theology as liberation, as critical thinking, and as an approach to New Testament studies."[34] Ironically, she had more Roman Catholic women students at the Episcopal Divinity School than she did at Notre Dame—a Catholic university. And her successes extended beyond the classroom.

In 1985, the Society of Biblical Literature elected her as its first female president. This election recognized the serious and transformative contributions Dr. Schüssler Fiorenza's academic work had made to the field of biblical studies. It affirmed that, as a whole, although many might not have agreed with her theoretical ideas, they still admired and recognized her academic ability and her original way of thinking. It also provided her with a platform from which to make other scholars aware of critical feminist issues within biblical studies.

In the same year, Elisabeth Schüssler Fiorenza and Judith Plaskow originated the *Journal of Feminist Studies in Religion*, which some have deemed a trailblazing academic journal. Schüssler Fiorenza recalled that the seed for this idea was sown in 1972 at the Women Doing Theology Conference, where she met Judith Plaskow. Over the years, their friendship grew and their dialogue about religion and feminist issues grew with it. Finally, in the early 1980s, Plaskow said to Schüssler Fiorenza, "Either we do something about it [the feminist journal] or we stop talking about it."[35] So, Elisabeth Schüssler Fiorenza and Judith Plaskow each took a large personal and financial risk, and began developing the journal. As they pondered the journal's mission, they decided they needed to find an independent press. They wanted the journal to be as free as possible from commercial constraint or censorship. Of course, very few major biblical or religious journals at that time had much interest in fostering the development of a feminist competitor to their male-dominant academic monopoly. So, Schüssler Fiorenza and Plaskow proceeded independently.

As they developed their philosophy and practices for the *Journal of Feminist Religious Studies*, both Plaskow and Fiorenza agreed upon several principles. First, they agreed on a critical feminist orientation for the journal that would go beyond gender. From the outset they defined women not by gender alone, but also by race, social position, economic status, and a variety of other factors. Next, they agreed that the journal should be a "venue [for academic feminists] to publish their innovative work."[36] Because feminist writing was, and often still is, seen as ideological in the negative sense of the word, journals that operate under the pretense of value neutrality rarely publish feminist articles. In an academic atmosphere of "publish or perish," Plaskow and Fiorenza knew they and the next generation of feminist thinkers needed a place to publish. Finally, wanting to provide more than just a place to publish, Plaskow and Fiorenza agreed that the *Journal of Feminist Religious Studies* should provide a forum for discussing feminist religious issues. Both Plaskow and Fiorenza knew that for the field of feminist religious studies to grow, a place for the free and vibrant interchange of ideas would be needed. Both agreed that the journal should be open to the views of many different religions and disciplines, and open to a broad spectrum of ideas while adhering to the highest academic standards. Both believed, and the journal has demonstrated, that these high academic standards could be maintained without perpetuating dominant male academic structures.

Because feminist theorists include and even privilege women's experience as a foundation and starting point of theoretical inquiry and/or debate, feminist writing often finds itself criticized for its supposedly personal, and nondetached, ideological character. Elisabeth Schüssler Fiorenza tells the story of Katie G. Cannon, who wrote an outstanding paper entitled "The Agony of Jesus in the Garden of Gethsemane." When she submitted the paper to her professor, he acknowledged its academic merits, but then rejected it because it moved him emotionally. He ordered her to rewrite the paper, so she "bleached and neutered" herself to meet his positivist, value-neutral expectations.[37] The *Journal of Feminist Studies in Religion*, therefore, provided a place for academically high quality feminist writing that might not fit into the kyriarchal structures of the traditional male academic system.

The founding of the *Journal of Feminist Religious Studies* created opportunities for feminist and women scholars and writers. Schüssler Fiorenza points out that many feminist writers who got their start in the journal received book deals as a result. It has proved to be a catalyst for feminist religious studies, helped advance the careers of feminist thinkers and

PUBLISH OR PERISH, BUT DON'T DARE MAKE ME FEEL ANYTHING

In the male-dominated world of academia, in order to rise to the top of one's field, or even secure a moderately well-paying job as a professor, a person needs to understand and heed the truism, "publish or perish!" Unfortunately, the number of published papers in "quality" academic journals often becomes a more important criterion for hiring a professor than that person's ability to teach or to motivate students to learn. Feminist women face this, but they also face the difficulty of obtaining approval for their academic papers from kyriocentric professors. Because feminist biblical inter-pretation begins with personal experience, it often is infused with *both* stereotypical academic rigor *and* an acknowledgment of human emotion. It is frequently questioned, therefore, and far too often rejected as "not objective" and "not academic." This marginalizes women in academia. It also, from time to time, baffles male professors who experience it.

As an example, Schüssler Fiorenza, during an interview, offered a story told by Katie G. Cannon, a womanist ethicist who has served on the editorial board of the *Journal of Feminist Studies in Religion* from its inception: "By way of personal anecdote, a world-renowned white male scholar once ranted and raved in his critique of my work, 'How dare you make me feel! . . . I should be able to read this paper and not feel anything!' And because my paper evoked feelings, which appeared to be a threat to this man's person and his intellectual property, the professor concluded that such an embodied paper was so bad that he could not even flunk it. Ironically, the focus of my paper was "The Agony in Gethsemane." So this world-renowned scholar insisted that I, an allegedly unqualified inferior woman of African descent, must master his dispassionate style. Painstakingly I rewrote tedious drafts, until I learned how to disassociate and become disembodied. I bleached and neutered myself so that I could write inert dense, oblique prose from the neck up. Yes, this senior professor believed, like so many powerbrokers today, the damnable lie that so-called academic rigor and scholarly excellence equal value-free, dispassionate, color-blank, experience-distant, mathematically calculated objectivity."

Source: Bucciarelli, Moira. "Q and A with Elisabeth Schüssler Fiorenza," Society of Biblical Literature Forum. Available online at *http://www.sbl-site.org/Article.aspx?ArticleId=68*

theorists, and given voice to thinkers and scholars too often marginalized by traditional academics.

Perhaps the journal's greatest contribution, however, rests in the record it produces of the debates, knowledge, and theories of feminist religious thinkers. As Elisabeth Schüssler Fiorenza often remarks, when she began formulating her critical feminist theories, she, and others as well, had to literally invent the field because kyriarchal power structures rarely see the need to record the ideas of women. She stresses that this need for reinvention arose because theories and ideas about kyriarchal systems of oppression that women had developed in the past had been erased from history. The *Journal of Feminist Religious Studies*, therefore, might help prevent the erasure of feminist theories for the next generation, allowing them to reach back to the ideas of their foremothers for guidance and support.

Elisabeth Schüssler Fiorenza also took her talents to Harvard University. In contrast to her ideological struggles with the entire system at the University of Notre Dame, she indicates Harvard Divinity School hired her because of her interest in feminist theory. Still, she admits, that although she is now at the center of the "academic core," she probably had more impact on the church at Notre Dame and the Episcopal Divinity School. She points out that, even though Harvard supports her, "emancipatory interests are still considered to be extreme."[38] Just what are these extreme views? She summarized them nicely in a recent interview when she said "I want a new earth and I want it passionately. It would be that everybody would have enough to live, everybody would have their dignity, everyone would be able to do what they want to do."[39] Then this professor who works in an important center of academic achievement, who once sat alone in the cold waiting for a care package that never came, mused and admitted, "I realize how privileged I am."[40] Indeed, though she struggled against kyriarchal systems, she never forgot those less fortunate than herself. Today she continues to champion their cause.

3

The Challenge of
In Memory of Her

*And truly I say to you, wherever the gospel
is preached in the whole world, what she
has done will be told in memory of her.*

The Gospel of Mark

A s Elisabeth Schüssler Fiorenza points out, when she and a few other women began formulating the field of feminist theology and hermeneutics, they had no preestablished methodology upon which to base their inquiries. The methods that provided foundational support for traditional academic disciplines, especially in the field of biblical studies, developed out of kyriocentric ideologies that are at odds with feminist and liberation thinking. Further, Schüssler Fiorenza centered her efforts not only on the kyriocentric structures of the academic world, but also on the role of women in churches. Since much of church teaching and authority was, and still is, based upon methods of interpreting the Bible that were harmful to women, Schüssler Fiorenza saw the need to address this issue as well.

In Memory of Her, therefore, challenges both the academic pretense of value-neutral, scientific hermeneutical methods and the church's claim that the Bible speaks with the very voice and authority of God, and so does the church when it quotes the Bible to support its positions. One often hears this in the form, "The Bible says 'X,'" with "X" usually being someone's preconceived notion of how things really ought to be. Schüssler Fiorenza aimed her book at both the academic world and the religious world. In the introduction to the tenth anniversary edition of *In Memory of Her*, however, she admits some trepidation over how each audience would accept or reject her "feminist rhetoric."[41] With publication of the book, however, she hoped to shift both the academic and religious vision of biblical studies and interpretation, so she could not take the safe route.

Books about females in the Bible were, and still are, popular. These books, however, tended to perpetuate kyriarchal structures by analyzing women in the Bible in kyriocentric terms. In other words, Schüssler Fiorenza rejected the notion that a book *about* females must automatically be a feminist work. She asserted that one cannot consider a book feminist unless its underlying ideology argues against kyriocentrism and for the well-being of women. Simply because the content of a book deals with females does not make its contents feminist. Had

Schüssler Fiorenza written a safe book, devoid of controversy, about the lives of females in the Bible, she might still be teaching at the University of Notre Dame. Instead, she wrote a book that has begun to reshape biblical studies.

The difference between a book about females in the Bible and *In Memory of Her* rests in Schüssler Fiorenza's methodology. The first three chapters of the book, which taken together she labels "Seeing-Naming-Reconstructing," explore and analyze, among other things, various paradigms of hermeneutics, the androcentric nature of biblical texts and how they became authoritative, and what reconstructive remedies and methods feminist interpreters might develop in order to counteract these problems. The remainder of the book is often misinterpreted. In it, Schüssler Fiorenza offers a fairly comprehensive example of how her critical feminist reconstructive method of biblical interpretation works. In doing so, she analyzes at length the role of women in the Bible. She looks at how the writers of the Bible, and later biblical interpreters, obscured and erased much of that role before reconstructing it so that it could again be seen and appreciated. She demonstrates that, far from insignificant victims, women played major roles in the early Christian church and the formation of the Christian religion.

All too often, however, this is seen as Schüssler Fiorenza's attempt to recover an idyllic picture of early Christianity in which women shared absolute equality with men. Ironically, Schüssler Fiorenza explicitly warns against this at the end of the methodological chapters in her book. She argues that her work should "not be misread as that of a search for true, pristine, orthodox beginning."[42] She describes her interpretational model as one of "social interaction and religious transformation, of Christian 'vision' and historical realization, of struggle for equality and against patriarchal domination."[43] Schüssler Fiorenza is arguing that her feminist model of historical reconstruction does not necessarily aim at finding the exact portrait of early Christianity to use as a comparison to the situation today. Instead, her model offers instead a critical and methodological

ELISABETH
SCHÜSSLER
FIORENZA

Elisabeth is about five years old in this picture, taken in 1943. Her brother, Nikolaus (left), is two years younger. The following year, Elisabeth and her family would move from Romania to Germany.

Young Elisabeth is about nine years old here. The photograph, taken in 1947, shows Elisabeth in her first communion outfit. At the time, she was just two years away from becoming a student at the Humanistiches Gymnasium, where she would study classical languages and literature.

A sixteen- or seventeen-year-old Elisabeth (left), has the role of "princess" in a play. The princess's "governess" (right) peers through her spectacles.

At nineteen, Elisabeth is just one year away from finishing her studies at the Humanistisches Gymnasium. The following year, in 1958, she would begin studying theology at the University of Würzberg.

Elisabeth, seated in the center, is shown with (from left to right) her mother, her partner Francis, her brother Nikolaus, and her father. The family had gathered to celebrate Christmas of 1965.

Elisabeth, second from left, poses with (left to right) her father, Francis, and her mother, for this photograph, taken in 1965. The year before, Elisabeth had moved to Münster to pursue a research position at the university there. It was in Münster that she met Francis, who would become her husband and a distinguished theologian in his own right.

Elisabeth, now an assistant professor of theology at the University of Notre Dame, is hard at work preparing for her classes. During this same year, in 1971, she also agreed to co-chair the women's caucus of the Society of Biblical Literature with Carol Christ.

A neighborhood babysitter looks on while Elisabeth walks with her daughter, Chris, who was born in 1973. Elisabeth juggled the responsibilities of motherhood with a full-time professorship at the University of Notre Dame.

In 1977 Elisabeth Schüssler Fiorenza was an associate professor of theology at the University of Notre Dame. Just five years earlier, her dissertation was published in German.

In 1980, around the time this photo was taken, Elisabeth Schüssler Fiorenza became a full professor of theology at the University of Notre Dame. She would continue teaching there until 1984.

Elisabeth, seated second from the left, attends a 1985 conference in Austria. The trip was one of many that make up her extensive experience in workshops and lectures concerning critical feminist interpretations of the Bible.

By the time this photo was taken in 1990, Elisabeth had been a Krister Stendahl professor at the Divinity School of Harvard University for two years. Her distinguished teaching career in the United States began twenty years earlier at the University of Notre Dame.

Elisabeth received an honorary doctorate from the University of Würzberg, her alma mater, in 2000. The following year, *Wisdom Ways: Introducing Feminist Biblical Interpretation* would be published. Her intent was to redefine the antifeminist messages perceived in the Bible and make way for a more inclusive doctrine that embraces all Christians equally, regardless of gender.

lens through which to recover and reconstruct the struggles of women in the Jesus movement. These struggles were almost, but not quite, erased both by the kyriarchal concerns and androcentric language of the New Testament writers themselves and later, the interpreters of the texts.

To recover and reconstruct the struggle of women in early Christianity, therefore, means to challenge what Schüssler Fiorenza calls the erroneous, but common, assumptions of kyriocentric thinking. For example, many assume that women do not appear very often in the New Testament. It seems to make sense that women, who are assumed to have played only a minor role in history itself, would also then have played only a minor role in the development of Christianity. On the contrary, Schüssler Fiorenza shows that women were prophets, apostles, and leaders in early Christianity. For example, over one-third of the list of Paul's coworkers in Romans 16 is made up of women. Junia, perhaps best exemplifies the problem Schüssler Fiorenza's feminist reconstructive method seeks to remedy.

The central question surrounding the name Junia is whether or not Junia is a female or male name. If it is female, as it seems most likely to be, then in the text of the Epistle to the Romans the apostle Paul addresses a female as an apostle. This, of course, does not make sense to, nor does it please, those of a kyriocentric mindset. To understand the issue surrounding Junia, a female name from the first century, we need to understand that the Bible as we find it on bookshelves today is actually the result of long and detailed labors done by scholars who pieced together ancient manuscripts, fragments, and parchments. The textual question of how to translate the name Junia comes up again and again because the manuscript evidence does not lend itself to a unanimous opinion. Again, the central question is whether or not to translate Junia as a male or female name. Although scholars can find no other example in first century literature that would give credence to translating it as a male name, several scholars on one of the most influential academic committees thought it unlikely to be a female name. Why? Not because the manuscript evidence supported translating it as a male name. It did not. Not because the name was used in other ancient sources to refer to a male. It was not. But solely because the members of the committee—coming at the problem from an androcentric mindset—thought it unlikely that Paul would recognize a female as an apostle. The kyriocentric attitudes of the committee, therefore, exemplify the need for Schüssler Fiorenza's feminist reconstructive method and her critical feminist hermeneutic of liberation.

Although we will look at this method in much greater detail later, there is one particular characteristic of Schüssler Fiorenza's method that should be emphasized here. Her feminist reconstructive method is a "model of ongoing conflict and struggle between kyriarchal domination and radical democratic structures and worldviews—a struggle that runs squarely through ancient and modern history."[44] Thus, Schüssler Fiorenza's method does not, in *In Memory of Her*, concretize a view of women in Christianity. Instead she shatters the concrete assumptions of those who would use the Bible and biblical interpretation to uphold oppressive structures of domination. For those who benefit from oppressive power structures, therefore, the book seemed dangerous enough to attack on any front. For others, mainly those oppressed by kyriarchal structures of domination, the book provided a needed tool to help them expose and oppose the oppression that harmed them.

Indeed, although Elisabeth Schüssler Fiorenza worried about reaction to the book from both academia and members of the clergy, she received positive feedback from some elements in both communities. When she wrote the introduction to the tenth anniversary edition of *In Memory of Her*, Schüssler Fiorenza included a variety of stories of women who found the tools to empower themselves to resist kyriarchal structures of domination. For example, she tells the story of a group of African-American Pentecostal women ministers who came to a workshop on *In Memory of Her* entitled "Prophets, Teachers, Founders" because they were founders of a "house church" that offered shelter to women newly released from prison.[45] The male pastor of the church from which they had made their "exodus" felt "threatened," "campaigned against them," and challenged "their legitimacy on biblical grounds."[46] These women would not be intimidated, however. Their understanding of *In Memory of Her* provided them with a critical feminist interpretive framework that did not see the Bible as the authoritative "Word of God," but instead as "documents of the struggle between the early Christian practice of equality and that of patriarchal submission."[47] These women did not bend to the kyriarchal attempt at domination. Instead, they found themselves empowered to continue their leadership in their house church, along with their service to former prisoners trying to construct a new life. *In Memory of Her* has inspired some to develop what Schüssler Fiorenza calls an "ekklēsia of wo/men" as an alternative to the kyriarchy of their androcentric churches. We will return to this theme in the last chapter of this book.

In Memory of Her also provided for those without it access to a solid theological education. For numerous women, the book provided an opportunity to achieve an academically solid understanding of biblical studies. Those willing to explore *In Memory of Her* with diligence and effort seemed to find it an education in itself. For example, one group of women without formal biblical or theological education tells of how they read the book one page at a time, and with a dictionary, "acquired a thorough biblical theological education."[48] After completing *In Memory of Her*, this study group wrote to Dr. Schüssler Fiorenza to ask if she could recommend an "equally difficult" systematic theology.[49] Since the book's publication, those willing to engage Schüssler Fiorenza's ideas seem to find a way to understand *In Memory of Her*, despite its academically rigorous style. By contrast, Schüssler Fiorenza notes that often it is academics who are unwilling to even entertain the possible plausibility of her feminist theoretical ideas, and will instead complain that the book is hard to understand. The history of how *In Memory of Her* has been critiqued and received is very telling. It seems to indicate that those privileged by the status quo tend to regard the book negatively while those who are oppressed by the kyriarchal structures described within it tend to regard the book with deep appreciation, despite the manifestly academic tone of Schüssler Fiorenza's writing.

Despite the academic world's mixed reaction to *In Memory of Her*, the work has received a great deal of scholarly attention. Its theories have been applied to a variety of fields outside of biblical theological studies including rhetoric, linguistics, sociology, psychology, and history. But while *In Memory of Her* has received much attention, it has nevertheless been labeled by the academic establishment as a "women's studies" book. *In Memory of Her*, therefore, is often marginalized. Although most scholars find the book provocative and challenging, many view the book as a nonstandard example of scholarship, a work outside the norm, and a text that does not meet the normal criteria for broad application and use in college classrooms. Remember that even Schüssler Fiorenza herself was not allowed to use the book while teaching at the University Notre Dame. Still, many scholars, often hostile to Schüssler Fiorenza's ideas, have used her work to bolster their own careers. Schüssler Fiorenza notes that many scholars have "summarized, taken over, built on, expanded, or exploited the book's arguments and research materials in different ways."[50] The book's overall message is often misunderstood.

To understand the central premise of *In Memory of Her*, we need to understand what it is not. Although *In Memory of Her* does attempt to reconstruct the sociological, historical, and theological setting of early Christianity, it does not claim to simply follow the so-called "value-neutral" approach of most biblical scholars. Indeed, it flatly rejects this approach. Schüssler Fiorenza chooses to see women as central, not "peripheral" to the early church.[51] This creates a lens through which Schüssler Fiorenza interprets early church history. The difference between her and her critics, however, is that Schüssler Fiorenza freely admits the nature of the lens she uses. Those who claim to attempt to see things "as they really were" do not admit their own biases nor those of early Christianity. Thus, Schüssler Fiorenza, and most feminist biblical scholars, tend to admit the ideological shape of the lenses they use to interpret the Bible. Unfortunately, critics of feminist interpreters usually claim the lenses they use are objective or neutral, when, in fact, they too have ideological bents to them. Often, the criticism sticks, however, because the dominant forces in society see feminism as ideological, and traditional biblical hermeneutics as normative, or even scientific. Schüssler Fiorenza has fought this misperception since she began her academic career.

Schüssler Fiorenza further explains her lens when she argues that although women in early Christianity did suffer oppression and were often marginalized, they nevertheless were "historical agents who . . . produced, shaped, and sustained social life in general and early Christian socio-religious relations in particular."[52] This is not an idealized view of the contributions of women within early Christianity, nor is it an idealization of early Christianity itself. Schüssler Fiorenza does not attempt to reconstruct the histories of this period in order to offer a utopian counterinterpretation. *In Memory of Her* instead attempts to uncover the story of women's struggles to overcome kyriocentric power structures, especially the manner in which these struggles occurred in early Christianity. Schüssler Fiorenza argues that *In Memory of Her* is not a projection of positive "assumptions of wo/men's dignity, agency, and centrality back into the past."[53] For Schüssler Fiorenza, the standard methods of interpreting history and religious contexts actually do project assumptions onto the past, but rarely, if ever, admit those assumptions. Those who admit their ideological assumptions such as Schüssler Fiorenza in *In Memory of Her,* are often labeled as not being neutral by those unwilling to admit that they themselves do not practice total neutrality. Schüssler Fiorenza's reconstruction of early Christianity in *In Memory of Her,* therefore, claims neither to be an idealized portrait of a better time for women nor a so-called value-neutral reinterpretation of standard characterization of the period. Instead, Schüssler Fiorenza sees her work as an attempt to recover the memory of the struggle against the kyriarchal power structures that oppressed and marginalized women during the early formation of Christianity and beyond.

To understand Schüssler Fiorenza's argument, one must understand that history is not simply a value-neutral record of events. It is instead a human interpretation of other people's memories. Because no interpretation is wholly neutral, Schüssler Fiorenza believes those who attempt to write about history need to admit and critique their own interpretational frameworks or points of view in an open, honest manner. Perhaps the best statement of Schüssler Fiorenza's ideological framework in *In Memory of Her* comes from the introduction to the book's tenth anniversary edition.

She freely informs her readers of the "feminist-liberationist premise [that informs] *In Memory of Her.*"[54] The feminist-liberationist premise of the book, then, leads to several themes or goals that permeate the work. Schüssler Fiorenza, in *In Memory of Her* seeks to accomplish the following:

- "interrupt" and debunk the idea that history lends itself to one, clear-cut, authoritative interpretation of its events and ideas;

- transform society by challenging the notion that women are naturally unimportant to history because they were not major participants in historical events;

- reconstruct history so that it strengthens people's resolve to battle societal and religious structures of oppression and to fight for their dignity and rights, even if doing so seems to run counter to the prevailing ideology of their societies;

- show that the battle for liberation and dignity must involve the questioning of the traditional methods used to write history and thereby maintain the status quo.[55]

In other words, for Schüssler Fiorenza, the manner in which history is presently written, although it claims to be neutral, actually contributes to dominant power structures that harm women. Thus, Schüssler Fiorenza argues that "[d]ignity and self-respect, the question of the oppression and rights as well as emancipatory struggle are the key to the epistemological/ hermeneutical framework of meaning that determine the book's feminist critical reconstruction of early Christian beginnings."[56]

Schüssler Fiorenza's interpretational method seeks both to challenge the standard interpretations based on an assumption of neutrality and to reconstruct early Christian history by centering attention on women's struggles against oppression. Schüssler Fiorenza places *In Memory of Her* "within liberation theories and theologies in general, and feminist epistemologies and interpretive practices in particular. It is inspired by theoretical work rooted in liberation movements around the globe."[57] It has been translated into numerous languages and has received warm welcome from those who struggle against oppression. Although Schüssler Fiorenza aligns her interpretational stance with women and their struggles for liberation, she also sets out specific methods of interpretation which have proven useful for feminist and liberation biblical scholars ever since the first publication of *In Memory of Her*.

Since interpreting history through the lens of what Schüssler Fiorenza calls a critical feminist hermeneutic of liberation means challenging standard interpretational techniques, she needed to create an alternative methodology. Her explanation of these methods in *In Memory of Her* reflects her early ideas concerning biblical interpretation. In the next chapter, we will examine the principles of her full program of interpretation in some detail. In *In Memory of Her*, however, as she explains in the introduction to the tenth anniversary edition, her first step in her "model of feminist historical-theological reconstruction . . . seeks to interrupt and change dominant interpretive discourses."[58] She suggests that *In Memory of Her* provides an example of how to accomplish this.

First, in *In Memory of Her*, Schüssler Fiorenza centers her efforts on "destabilizing linguistic frames of meaning."[59] To understand what she means, consider the abbreviations "Mr.," "Mrs.," and "Miss." Each one functions as a societal title. These titles seem so familiar that they tend to make sense to most people. But if we challenge their validity and examine them more closely, we will see that they are actually formed with androcentric language used to support kyriarchal structures of domination. While "Mr." might refer to a married man or a single man, the women's titles all indicate the relationship a woman has with a man. "Mrs." is a term reserved for a woman married to a man. "Miss" is a term for a woman not married to a man. In both cases, the standard language that society uses sees women only in terms of their relationship to a man. Countless other instances exist that demonstrate the male-centered nature of language: "mankind," "fireman," or, "God the Father," for example. While these are examples of modern male biases in language, Schüssler Fiorenza points out that the very language used to speak about women in the Bible itself was also tainted with androcentrism by male writers who wrote from a kyriarchal point of view.

For Schüssler Fiorenza, this has at least two negative consequences for women. First, women, as they appear in the biblical texts and as they are interpreted by biblical scholars, are generally seen only in relationship to the men around them. They do not stand as independent and active agents of history. Second, the androcentric language used creates an assumption that women were so marginalized that they were not important in the actual flow and creation of history. Schüssler Fiorenza argues that, contrary to these assumptions, women did indeed contribute to history and helped to shape early Christianity. The androcentric language of the biblical texts and the biblical interpretations, however, tends to minimize their contributions. Thus, the history of the early Christianity must be reconstructed to include the contributions of women and their struggle against oppression. For Schüssler Fiorenza, this is not meant to idealize women, but to come to a more plausible and less harmful understanding of early Christian origins.

Schüssler Fiorenza warns, however, against simply writing about women in the Bible rather than reconstructing early Christianity to include women's struggles against oppression. To simply write about women from an assumption of value-neutrality often leads to writers perpetuate the androcentric language Schüssler Fiorenza seeks to interrupt. Just because a book is about women does not mean that it is a critical feminist interpretation or that it challenges the status quo.

The second academically and socially dominant idea Schüssler Fiorenza wants to interrupt is the "positivist figuration of history."[60] Here Schüssler Fiorenza wants to expose the false nature of the idea that history is like a court reporter's "transcript."[61] Because no one who is alive today actually witnessed the events of early Christianity—and even if they did, their account would still be an interpretation of what they witnessed—no actual account of what really happened exists. Many biblical scholars assume they can get closer to the actual reality of history if they only apply what they call objective, scientific methods to the problem. Most of the historical research done within biblical studies, however, centers on interpretation of documents that are tainted by androcentric language and kyriarchal concerns. Because of this, Schüssler Fiorenza argues that the process of interpretations cannot possibly be fully objective.

Yet, the assumption that biblical scholars should ideally apply objective methods of interpretation persists. Schüssler Fiorenza argues that this only makes the kyriocentrism inherent in the historical documents more concrete and more normative. This, in turn, simply perpetuates the kyriarchal power structures found in the ancient documents of Christianity.

If the documents are tainted, then, and the so-called objective approach to interpreting them is flawed, what can we do? Schüssler Fiorenza suggests that we take a middle path between, on the one hand, assuming that we can absolutely know what was "really said" or what "really happened,"[62] and, on the other hand, assuming we can know nothing about the character and essence of the historical period or movement we wish to study. To this end, Schüssler Fiorenza suggests that we understand the Jesus we find in the books of biblical scholars and historians as a *remembered Jesus*, one who is the product of interpretation. Further, she argues that we should also see the Jesus found in the early texts of Christianity as a remembered Jesus who has been modified by the interpretational memories and ideological biases of those who created the texts.

The primary reason Schüssler Fiorenza wants to interrupt the assumption of objectivity in biblical and historical studies, however, centers on the authority assumed by scholars and others who assert the legitimacy of their assumedly objective methods. Schüssler Fiorenza argues that "[c]laiming scientific accuracy and status for their own interpretations allows scholars and journalists both to remain silent about the ethico-political premises and interests of their own work and to conceal the ideological and disciplinary pressures of those scholarly or popular interpretive communities for whom they write."[63] She addresses not only academics but also popular writers. She asserts that the "discourses of *In Memory of Her* seek to interrupt not only the positivistic [those who assume objectivity] ethos of historical scholarship but also journalistic accounts that popularize it."[64] In essence, Schüssler Fiorenza wishes to expose the assumption that simply claiming objectivity for oneself or the text does not negate the presence of underlying ideological biases both in the interpreter and in the biblical text itself.

The third way Schüssler Fiorenza attempts in *In Memory of Her* to interrupt dominant interpretive discourses is by "questioning reconstructive methods and models."[65] She argues that biblical studies and biblical historical studies have been in the past, and are most often still, written by "elite powerful men [who] write history on the basis of their own experiences and interests."[66] Knowing who engages in biblical studies is important because if only one dominant type of person makes the effort, then it is likely that only one general view of the world will emerge from the study. Thus, because most biblical scholars have been—and mostly still are—elite white men, the views of elite white men tend to predominate as the main "flavor" of biblical studies. This, however, provides only one general lens through which to look at the biblical world and early Christianity.

Think of it this way. Imagine an elite white male, raised in relative comfort, who goes to the best prep schools, then goes to an Ivy League university, and then becomes a professor at, for example, Yale. Then imagine a poor woman who has struggled all her life just to survive, to feed herself and her children, and who has received a substandard education with little hope of going to college. Each will have a different way of looking at the world, existence, and their life. Perhaps the man sees history as a steady progression under the logical and rational authority of God-ordained men. Meanwhile, the woman might see history as a cruel joke perpetrated and maintained by those who are rich, powerful, and willing to oppress others to remain so. If a person's present way of looking at the world is kyriocentric, then their vision of the past will likely be as well. Even if this lens seems value-neutral, it is not, because it was constructed in a kyriarchal world.

Schüssler Fiorenza's main concern with our different methods and models of understanding history centers on the assumption that the kyriocentric way of seeing the world is quite often seen as normal, while other ways of seeing the world are dismissed as ideological and biased. The male-centered nature of society, our language, and, specifically, biblical interpretation must, for Schüssler Fiorenza, not be seen as the normal way of viewing the world. This brings up some complex, difficult questions. Why is the male considered the "norm" and the female the "other"? Why, at least until quite recently, are pronouns generally masculine in everyday language use? Why, Schüssler Fiorenza asks, is it assumed that males should rule and females should serve? Without delving into her answer too deeply, Schüssler Fiorenza asserts that this issue has its origins in Western society's reliance on the ideas of ancient Greek philosophers, especially Aristotle, as normative guides. Aristotle argued that free, wealthy men were of a superior nature to women, and thus, by the laws of nature, were entitled to rule. Schüssler Fiorenza sees this idea popping up in the behavioral codes of the apostle Paul. Because the Bible is considered normative, society often sees Aristotle's assumption about men naturally ruling over women as normative as well, especially when transmitted through the authority of the Bible.

Schüssler Fiorenza questions why this kyriocentric hierarchy is still accepted as "the norm." She points out that those who hold to it often find themselves defending it with rather strained, and often implausible logic. For example, she points out that the patriarchalism of Aristotle works its way into the Pauline tradition in the form of "love-patriarchalism," or, patriarchalism that is believed to be for the best benefit of both the men who are at the top of the hierarchy and the women whom they are to protect and love, or, to put it bluntly, rule. The idea here is that women, because of their inherently inferior nature, are incapable of deciding things for themselves or taking care of themselves. The man must step in and, for the good of the woman, rule. Schüssler Fiorenza digs beneath this logic, however, and asks why the argument for patriarchalism, in any form, needs to exist at all. Why must Aristotle and Paul exert so much effort to defend it, especially if it is supposed to be obvious? She discerns that the argument must be made in the face of opposition, often lost or forgotten under kyriocentric biases of those who write the histories, that challenges the sense of the hierarchal system. As she puts it, "explicit kyriocentric arguments become necessary only when kyriarchal oppression is no longer common sense."[67] These assumptions of natural male rule and privilege, Schüssler Fiorenza argues, must be, and have been, challenged and exposed, both in the interpretations of biblical scholars and in the texts of the Bible itself.

Thus far, Schüssler Fiorenza's methods of interpreting biblical texts have focused on preventing or critiquing long-established ideologies and assumptions. Her fourth method of interpretation, however, provides an antidote to these problems: "elaborating a reconstructive model of struggle."[68] For example, Schüssler Fiorenza wishes to introduce a "radical democratic vision of self-determination in all areas of socio-cultural and religious life."[69] This vision is egalitarian and invites everyone, male and female, to participate. She argues against framing this vision in terms of gender, asserting instead that it is a vision meant for all. To

ARISTOTLE'S VIEW OF WOMEN

Throughout history, Western thinking has traditionally viewed the kyriocentric idea that men should rule over women as a given. Not until the twentieth century did females and slaves obtain the right to vote in the United States, and even then only after a bitter political battle and a constitutional amendment. Each Sunday morning, millions of Americans go to houses of worship where they are taught that wives should submit to their husbands, a teaching based upon their interpretation of the Household Codes of Paul. Where did these attitudes originate? They came, at least in part, from the philosophy of Aristotle.

In the *Politics of Aristotle*, the ancient philosopher sets out what he believes would be the ideal social/political pattern for humans to adopt. His ideas are blatantly hierarchal. The only group of humans he sees fit to govern are elite, wealthy men. He bases his argument on the assumption that elite men, by nature of their status and gender, have been given a character that is superior to women. He argues, "For the male, unless constituted in some respect contrary to nature, is by nature more expert in leading than the female."

He further argues that the "ruling and the ruled" are set in society by nature, "for the free person rules the slave, the male the female, and the man the child."

So for Aristotle, one of the West's most influential philosophical and political giants, women are ruled by men, not because of social inequity or kyriocentric bias, but because it is only natural. Aristotle's ideas have been enormously influential. They may also have had a profound influence on the Household Codes of the New Testament. The pattern, at the very least, mimics Aristotle's kyriocentric theory.

Source: Aristotle, *The Politics*, translated and with an introduction by Carnes Lord (Chicago: University of Chicago Press, 1984), Book One, Chapter 12, p. 52.

explain her conception of transforming what is generally known as the "church" she uses the word *ekklēsia* as an alternative. She points out that the English word "church" is based on a Greek word *kyriakē*, that means "belonging to the lord/master/father." On the other hand, the meaning of the Greek word ekklēsia would be translated as a "public assembly of the political community" or a "democratic assembly of full citizens."[70] The New Testament overwhelmingly favors the use of ekklēsia or assembly, but later kyriarchally-minded societies shifted the commonly used word to "church," which carried within it an assumption of patriarchal hierarchy.

By reconstructing and resurrecting the word ekklēsia, Schüssler Fiorenza opens more liberating possibilities for biblical interpretation. For example, Schüssler Fiorenza points out that the word ekklēsia suggests meeting in a private dwelling, a home. Women, in biblical times, were often given the charge of the home; therefore, we may reasonably assume that they played prominent roles in church leadership. Indeed, it is likely, Schüssler Fiorenza points out, that early Christianity may have attracted women into its fold for this very reason. The fact that the New Testament uses ekklēsia rather than kyriakē indicates that despite the often androcentric language of the biblical text, a socio-religious space existed as an opportunity for women to flourish as leaders within early Christianity. Schüssler Fiorenza is careful to point out, however, that Christianity was not the only socio-religious movement that garnered followers. It was one of many, especially within Judaism itself. Schüssler Fiorenza makes this point because she is concerned about the possibility of anti-Semitism within feminist biblical studies, something she warns against quite often. Nevertheless, we can see that to look at the biblical text from a critical feminist hermeneutic of liberation is to uncover shades of reality often hidden by kyriocentric language, assumptions, and ideological concerns.

Although she uses her emancipatory method of biblical interpretation to outline this vision, both Protestants and Catholics criticized Schüssler Fiorenza's methods. From the Protestant point of view, some argued that Schüssler Fiorenza sought to reconstruct a feminist utopia as her portrait of early Christianity. Schüssler Fiorenza continues to counter this charge by insisting that her model be used for uncovering the struggles of women to overcome oppression, not as a method of perpetuating positivist methods of interpretation. From the Catholic point of view, some argued that Schüssler Fiorenza intends to foster through her writings a female church of small group meetings. But Schüssler Fiorenza sees the ekklēsia not as a gendered reality, nor as a static and rigid formula, but instead as an "active process, moving toward greater equality, freedom, and responsibility as well as toward communal relations free of domination."[71] The form it takes, Schüssler Fiorenza insists, is not set. She sees this as a preexisting reality that has not yet fully realized itself or its potential. It is dynamic, organic, and alive, rather than structural, hierarchal, and stagnant.

Schüssler Fiorenza's critical feminist reconstruction of early Christian origins elicits criticism, which in turn affords her the opportunity to further explain her ideas. For example, she is sometimes criticized for using "a modern understanding of equality as [*In Memory of Her's*] interpretive lens."[72] As we noted earlier, no critical lens is purely without bias. So, the choice of lenses must be based upon criteria other than its ability to be objective, because that ability does not exist. Generally, in Schüssler Fiorenza's works, we see that the choice is most often between the pseudo-objective lenses that actually hide other unrecognized ideologies, or more open lenses, such as critical feminist theory, which readily admits its ideological stance and can defend it on grounds of ethics or human dignity. She argues that those who claim she insists on a modern lens of equality and justice in order to do biblical studies do not understand her methodology or her ideology. She does not want to reshape history to fit her preferred pattern of human freedom; on the contrary, she wants to trace and to learn from the struggles of women throughout history. She is particularly interested in women in the world of the biblical texts, who sought to resist kyriarchal and oppressive power structures. She rejects the idea of equality meaning "sameness," and argues instead that the "basic aim of *In Memory of Her* seeks to trace the struggles against kyriarchal relations of domination in the beginnings of early Christianity in the context of the Greco-Roman world to which Judaism belonged."[73] In other words, she traces the struggle, but does not insist on a dominant lens of modern equality or individualism.

Despite the necessity of defending *In Memory of Her* against those who misinterpret it or distort it for their own ends, Schüssler Fiorenza has developed in it the foundations of her theory of a critical feminist biblical hermeneutic of liberation. In doing so she reacquainted the reader not only with the concept of the church as an assembly, but also with the idea of *basileia,* or empire, as God's alternative world to the Roman and all other empires. The word basileia refers not only to the Roman or Greek kingdom or rule, but also to "an anti-Imperial . . . symbol that shapes oppositional imagination of the Jewish people victimized by the Roman imperial system."[74] Early Christians and Jews "dreamed of emancipation" from Roman imperial colonization. The Jewish people, from whom Jesus was born, were at the time of Jesus' birth under the oppressive rule of Rome. They had in the past fought against this rule, and indeed would again in the future. But during the life of Jesus they were simply oppressed by Rome. In this context, Schüssler Fiorenza points out that the "gospel of the basileia envisioned an alternative world free of hunger, poverty, and domination. . . . The basileia message of the Jesus movement found acceptance among the poor, the despised, the ill and possessed, the outcast, the prostitutes, and sinners, both men and women."[75] This is markedly different from the Roman and Greek kyriarchal understanding of basileia which opted for or assumed its legitimacy as a hierarchal, patriarchal system of power. Schüssler Fiorenza argues that the Jesus movement was one of several Jewish groups who fostered and dreamed of emancipation. Her reconstruction of the Jesus movement, she argues, is neither "fact" nor "ideal"

THE HOUSEHOLD CODES OF THE BIBLE

The New Testament and its interpretation have often been used by those in power to maintain their dominance over women, especially since it originated in a kyriarchal culture that used androcentric language. Of course, some texts tend to harm women more than others. One particularly problematic set of texts describes what scholars have named the "Household Codes." In the Pauline tradition and later New Testament tradition, these codes are found in Colossians 3:18-4:1; Ephesians 5:22-6:9; I Timothy 2:11-15, 5:3-8, 6:1-2 and Titus 2:2-10. In these texts the reader will find orders for wives to obey and submit to husbands and for slaves to obey their masters. Men and women of low social rank are generally advised and instructed, in a sense, to do their duty, know their place, and honor those whom God has put in authority over them.

Schüssler Fiorenza critiques these codes by noting that they do not reflect original Christian ideas, but mirror instead the political and social philosophy of the cultures from which they came. For example, she points out that scholars find the substance of these codes in kyriarchal philosophers such as Aristotle. In other words, the codes exemplify the New Testament writers' culturally conditioned attempt to bolster the kyriarchal power structures that place elite men at the top of the power pyramid. In terms of religion, however, because they appear in the New Testament, a set of documents deemed authoritative, they cause even more harm to women than the codes found in secular philosophy.

The Household Codes in the New Testament occur in text most scholars believe Paul himself did not actually write. This theory gains credence when one reads Galatians 3:28, a text in which Paul argues gender does not matter if a person is in Christ. Since all reputable biblical scholars agree that Paul wrote Galatians, later New Testament texts that seem to directly contradict it should be viewed as suspect.

Of course, for Schüssler Fiorenza, the real issue is whether the method of interpreting the Household Codes builds up or tears down the status and well-being of women. Seen through the lens of a critical feminist biblical interpreter, these codes emerge as examples of kyriocentrism and as warning signs not to take everything in the New Testament literally.

but instead an "active process moving toward greater equality, freedom, and responsibility, as well as toward communal relations free of domination."[76]

In essence, Schüssler Fiorenza's *In Memory of Her* argues for a different vision, one opposed to the kyriarchal power structures that oppress so many women. Even in how we define the word basileia as "kingdom," we find that the lens we use and the ideology that created it dramatically influence what we see. In terms of biblical studies, *In Memory of Her* demonstrates the hypocrisy of claiming one's methods of interpretation are objective. It points to an alternative approach, one that aims at fostering freedom and ending oppression. It argues for a vision of biblical religion that is stripped of kyriarchal structures of domination and infused with an active, participatory "religious process of democratization which is inspired by the basileia-vision of a world free of exploitation, domination, and evil."[77] Schüssler Fiorenza feels that "[i]f the book moves readers to engage in this ethos of struggle, it has more than achieved its goal."[78]

4

A Variety
of Biblical
Interpretations

*. . . becoming a feminist interpreter means shifting
your focus from biblical interpretation construed as
an ever better explanation of the text to biblical
interpretation as a tool for becoming conscious
of structures of domination and for understanding
visions of a radical democracy that are inscribed in
our own experience as well as in that of the texts.*

Elisabeth Schüssler Fiorenza,
Wisdom Ways: Introducing Feminist Biblical Interpretation

Although *In Memory of Her* brought Elisabeth Schüssler Fiorenza international recognition among biblical scholars, that recognition did not translate into automatic acceptance of her ideas. She had sparked, or at the very least fanned, the fires of a debate among biblical scholars that still exists today. Schüssler Fiorenza's insistence on using a critical feminist hermeneutic of liberation struck some scholars as too ideological. Other scholars relegated her and her work to the category of "women's studies." Over the years, however, Schüssler Fiorenza's numerous books, journal articles, and presentations have helped to create an alternative methodological field of biblical studies based on critical feminist interpretation. Most people outside biblical studies, however, do not know much about the traditional methods of biblical interpretation that Schüssler Fiorenza's works attempt to refute.

This chapter uses Schüssler Fiorenza's critique of traditional methods as a way to introduce those methods to the reader. The traditional methods of biblical interpretation generally fall into four categories: the Doctrinal–Revelatory Paradigm, the Scientific–Positivist Paradigm, the Hermeneutical–Cultural Paradigm, and the Rhetorical–Emancipatory Paradigm. Each of these approaches constitutes for Schüssler Fiorenza a different perspective. They are not simply a set of methods but rather representations of particular ways of looking at the world, and particularly biblical studies. One might even say that they are similar to belief systems. In order for each of them to work, the interpreter must accept certain assumptions about the particular paradigm's methodological approach. Some form of assumption always underlies an interpretational paradigm's methods; however, many interpreters find it difficult to understand or admit the assumptions upon which their methods are based. Most of the time these methodological paradigms of interpretation overlap. In other words, interpreters do not always use the same approach to interpretation in every situation. Once we have learned these approaches, we can understand how Schüssler

Fiorenza's critical feminist paradigm of interpretation relates to these other major systems.

THE DOCTRINAL–REVELATORY PARADIGM

This interpretational approach to the Bible assumes that the Bible is the "Word of God" divinely revealed, sometimes believed to be dictated by God to humans. The implications of such an assumption are staggering, although not often contemplated. In this paradigm, only a small gap, if any, exists between the very mind of God and the words on a page of the Bible. According to this paradigm, the Bible speaks with the authority of God. But the Bible does not really speak independently. Humans have to interpret it. While this paradigm of interpretation includes various methods to interpret the Bible, it leaves little room to challenge the authority of those interpretations. The interpreters within this paradigm often assume that their interpretations are based on and have the authority of the "Word of God."

This paradigm, when taken to its extreme, can lead to problems when different groups assume they have "correctly" interpreted the Bible. Think of the logic chain of this paradigm. If the Bible is the dictated "Word of God" to humans, then if humans "accurately" interpret the Bible, they too possess the authority of God based on the "Word of God." Schüssler Fiorenza points out that fundamentalist Christians often use similar logic to assert that their "understanding of religion and the Bible [as] the only approach that is truly Christian."[79] She points out, however, that this approach ignores the deep variety of methods this paradigm offers and limits the interpreter to "rationalist" modes of understanding.[80]

Perhaps the two greatest contributions of this paradigm of interpretation to biblical studies are the fourfold sense of Scripture from medieval Christianity and the PaRDeS method of interpretation from Judaism. In the fourfold sense of Scripture one first interprets a biblical text in a literal way (which actually means historical in this case); second in a moral manner; third, in a symbolic sense; and fourth, in a future looking/mystical manner. The PaRDeS method interprets the biblical texts from a variety of perspectives. The common sense, "plain sense of the text" is called *Peshat*; the allegorical sense is *Remez*; the more "legal and narrative" interpretations are *Derush*; and the "mystical" interpretation is *Sod*.[81] PaRDes is an acronym for all of these concepts. Within this paradigm both Judaism and Christianity find a variety of methods with which to interpret the biblical text, at least within the medieval period.

Along with these methods of interpretation, Schüssler Fiorenza points out several other characteristics of the Doctrinal–Revelatory Paradigm. In particular, under this paradigm, interpretations of the scriptures were often used as "proof texts" to uphold the doctrinal stance of the church. This paradigm was and is used to bolster authority based on the assumption that God's very words are behind various church edicts or doctrines. In a similar manner, when the Protestant Reformation took hold, scholars of the Reformation held to this paradigm's notion of divine revelation, but often insisted on one "correct" interpretation of the text. This interpretation was frequently expressed "in such a way as to confirm" rather than challenge a person's "pre-understanding" of the text.[82] When this singular interpretation is combined with divine, revelatory authority, the result, according to Schüssler Fiorenza, is far too often kyriocentric power structures that oppress and dominate women —with the assumed sanction and approval of God and "his Word." In other words, according to Schüssler Fiorenza, this paradigm assumes we can come close to, or even know, precisely what God said and what God meant. Of course, those who define what God said and what God meant are usually those already in kyriarchal positions of power. Arguing against their interpretations is generally seen as arguing against God's authority.

THE SCIENTIFIC–POSITIVIST PARADIGM

This model assumes at least two things. First, it assumes that a human interpreter can achieve objectivity when dealing with biblical texts. Second, it assumes that, much like the artifacts of archeology, there are facts buried deep in the layers of language and culture simply waiting to be discovered and learned. Schüssler Fiorenza points out that although this paradigm claims objectivity, it nevertheless is culturally conditioned, drawing its main inspiration from the Enlightenment and European academia. Europe at the time of the Enlightenment was fascinated with the ideas of science and the scientific process. The ideals of empiricism—relying on observation and experiment—were in the air, and scholars were drifting toward the assumption that only those things that could be observed were valid. The ancient religious and theological ideas of the church faced scrutiny they had not expected.

Schüssler Fiorenza points out that the aim of this paradigm was to approach the study of the Bible as scientifically as possible. Practitioners of this model assumed that there was a "chasm between the past and today" and searched for the "world behind the text."[83] Instead of basing the authority for its interpretations on the assumption of divine revelation, this paradigm claimed that it could prove the "facts" of what the Bible said, objectively, scientifically, and with a very high degree of certainty.

The Scientific–Positivist Paradigm, proposed as an antidote to the authority of the churches, viewed all theological, ideological, or religious presuppositions as nonscientific distortions of the meaning of the Bible. Even today, this paradigm sees all other paradigms as ideological while maintaining that it alone is objective and without bias. When confronted with ideological interpretational methods such as critical, emancipatory feminism, it simply claims that feminist theory is ideological while Scientific–Positivism is not. It argues that feminist theory distorts the plain and objective "facts" of the Bible as discovered by the Scientific–Positivist biblical scholars who have freed themselves from ideological bias.

Schüssler Fiorenza critiques many aspects of this paradigm. First, the claim of objectivity cannot be defended. All thoughts, ideas, and methodologies are products of, or at least influenced by, cultural conditioning. Simply claiming that one's own methodology is not culturally conditioned does not release one from the reality of personal or societal bias. As Schüssler Fiorenza puts it, Scientific–Positivism "denies its own particular Eurocentric perspectives and kyriarchal aims, which are indebted to the European Enlightenment."[84] By not admitting its own biases and ideologies, while at the same time criticizing other methodologies for their ideologies, Scientific–Positivism demonstrates its self-contradictory core. Even so, this paradigm is still reflected in academia, in churches, and often in popular opinion. Because of this, and because the "facts" that practitioners of this paradigm "discover" are often harmful to women, Schüssler Fiorenza's works often include arguments against its core assumptions.

THE HERMENEUTIC–CULTURAL PARADIGM

The Hermeneutic–Cultural Paradigm strikes at the core assumption of the Scientific–Positivist Paradigm: certainty. Rather than viewing biblical texts as data sets to be reviewed for facts, or representations of history to be scientifically interpreted in order to find their actual meaning, the Hermeneutic–Cultural Paradigm often "ascribes personified status to the text in order to construe it as a dialogue partner or . . . sees the text as a multicolored tapestry of meaning."[85] Unlike the first two paradigms, this one sees the biblical text not as an authoritative revelation or an ancient transcript of a culture, but rather as one of the " 'great books' or classics of Western culture, whose greatness does not consist in their accuracy as records of facts, but depends chiefly on their symbolic power."[86]

This paradigm is unconcerned with "dogmas [or] 'facts,' "[87] and sees instead the biblical text as having the potential to inspire many interpretations that say as much about the interpreter as they do about the biblical text itself. As Schüssler Fiorenza points out, this paradigm has been a "corrective" to the excesses of the Scientific–Positivist Paradigm of factual certainty.[88] For example, it argues that "there is no pure reason as instrument of knowledge that can lead to a just society. In the beginning there was not pure reason but power."[89] In other words, unlike the Scientific–Positivist Paradigm, this paradigm readily acknowledges the role of the interpreter as a creator, not just a discoverer of meaning. It further acknowledges that creators of meaning often produce meaning, not in order to follow the structures of reason, but instead to maintain their positions of power within a social or religious group.

Schüssler Fiorenza points out that this understanding of knowledge as created and manipulated, especially as articulated by feminist thinkers, undercuts societal assumptions about "the rights and knowledge of the modern elite male subject." These rights and knowledge of the "man of reason, were underwritten by the negation of such rights to devalued others, such as wives, children, slaves, aliens, natives, and other disenfranchised wo/men."[90] This paradigm, Schüssler Fiorenza argues, therefore intersects with colonial theory and its critique of modernity. In this sense, it improves on the first two paradigms; unfortunately, it is not sufficient.

The insufficiency of this paradigm rests in one of its core assumptions, that there is a "surplus of meaning" created by the interpretation of any text, an "endless play of meaning."[91] While this improves on the idea of only one fixed meaning authorized either by God or objective reasoning, it nevertheless opens the door to chaos. If all interpretations are possible, and all are equally plausible, then all interpretations are acceptable. Given this logic, the paradigm "eschews all truth claims."[92] No one biblical scholar can claim objective or revelatory certainty and authority for his or her interpretation. It is also true, however, that no one can reasonably claim that his or her interpretation has any more or less validity that that of another. This relativism, therefore, leaves in place the kyriarchal structures of domination set up by the other two paradigms. In doing so, this paradigm finds itself "incapable of addressing the increasing insecurities of globalized inequality."[93] It is also unable to foster movements for liberation that Schüssler

Fiorenza argues are needed to oppose kyriarchal power structures that oppress women.

THE RHETORICAL–EMANCIPATORY PARADIGM

It is within this paradigm that Schüssler Fiorenza places her critical feminist hermeneutics of liberation. We will address critical feminist methodology and assumptions in more detail in the next chapter. However, critical feminist biblical interpretation shares much with the other models within this paradigm. Indeed, this paradigm interests itself in the well-being of those who find themselves being subjugated by power relationships.

The most recent of all biblical interpretations, the Rhetorical–Emancipatory Paradigm brings together ideas and methods from hermeneutics, science, rhetoric, ethics, political theory and others. While it does not insist on one set interpretation authorized either by God or "the facts," it also does not adhere to the relativism of the Hermeneutic–Cultural Paradigm. Instead, its base is in the "long history [of] political-radical democratic struggles for emancipation."[94] It seeks to learn and discover the "ways in which biblical texts exercise influence and power in social and religious life."[95] In this case, the Bible is not a divinely revealed text given to uphold power structures, nor is it simply a data-mine one investigates to discover facts. It is more like a location, a place where competing societal and religious interests interact, and often enter into conflict.

Schüssler Fiorenza uses the term "rhetorical" to describe this paradigm because paramount to understanding how the biblical text functions is an understanding of the rhetorical context in which it functions. For the Rhetorical–Emancipatory Paradigm to work, one must consider that the meaning of the text, while not wholly certain or wholly uncertain, is "limited by [the] contexts"[96] in which it functions. In other words, "love your enemy" might mean one thing in the world of the truly wealthy and another in the world of abject poverty. In the world of the truly wealthy, perhaps one can afford to love even those considered to be enemies. But consider the sacrifice of loving those who deny poor men and women food, rights, and shelter. In the case of the wealthy, the biblical directive to love one's enemy might serve to improve the spiritual maturity of a person who follows the edict. On the other hand, in the case of those living in abject poverty, the biblical text might serve to dull and to lessen the potency of perhaps justifiable disgust with a person's lot in life. Thus, in the latter case, the biblical text would serve to persuade those who need to do so, *not* to rise up and demand the transformation of the social order. Notice that the same biblical text is used; nevertheless, the results, dependent on the rhetorical situation, have markedly different results. This exemplifies one of the basic assumptions of the Rhetorical-Emancipator Paradigm. Texts "function [either] to legitimate or challenge the status quo."[97] But their persuasive power is dependent on the rhetorical situation in which they function.

The goal of the Rhetorical–Emancipatory Paradigm is multi-faceted, but at its core, for Schüssler Fiorenza, it positions itself to empower women. As Schüssler Fiorenza puts it, "we insist that we who are the 'subordinated others' must engage in a political and theoretical process of constituting ourselves as subjects of knowledge and history. We have to use what we know about the world and about wo/men's lives for critiquing the Bible and biblical readings."[98] Schüssler Fiorenza, therefore, places women and their struggles at the center of her method-ological paradigm. Remember that all paradigms are ideological; therefore, perhaps the most significant criteria for judging them is, as Schüssler Fiorenza argues, whether or not they uphold or challenge the status quo.

For Schüssler Fiorenza, learning how to judge a particular theory is not a just a theoretical exercise; it is a vital imperative. If the dominant power structures remain in place and are allowed to harm women because they are upheld by academic or church-sanctioned interpretations of the Bible, then women will continue to suffer oppression that is somehow deemed justified in the name of the Bible. If women become aware not only of the difficulties they face but also of their power, Schüssler Fiorenza believes they hold within them the necessary energy to transform the world. To this end, Schüssler Fiorenza sets out her critical feminist hermeneutic of liberation, to which we now turn.

A Quilt of Many Colors

I want a new earth and I want it passionately. It would be that everybody would have enough to live, everybody would have their dignity, everyone would be able to do what they want to do.

Elisabeth Schüssler Fiorenza

A s we learned, Schüssler Fiorenza often likens her method of critical feminist biblical interpretation to dance, and prefers to use words that imply movement to describe it. But Schüssler Fiorenza is not limited by this metaphor. She also likens the field and practice of critical feminist biblical interpretation to the art of quilting, and even to a quilt itself. The quilt metaphor works particularly well to explain her methodology.

Quilts are made of various pieces, patterns, and fabrics. These pieces are then sewn together to form a single piece of cloth that provides the underlying foundation for the various pieces of the quilt. In the same way, Schüssler Fiorenza's critical feminist hermeneutic of liberation is composed of many rhetorical/hermeneutical methodologies. These ideas are sewn together by a common concern for the well-being of women and the elimination of kyriocentrism. They are based upon the idea that it is the critical feminist biblical interpreter, not a one-size-fits-all method, that underlies Schüssler Fiorenza's interpretational theory.

Rather than providing an interpretational method of the Bible that works every time, Schüssler Fiorenza's theory of biblical interpretation argues biblical interpretation is best performed by a transformed human who understands society's kyriarchal structures of domination, has the best interests of women in mind, and who, depending on the rhetorical situation, can use a variety of interpretational methods. After we look at the foundation of Schüssler Fiorenza's quilt, the critical feminist biblical interpreter, we will examine a variety of quilt squares she has sewn together to explain her theory.

CRITICAL FEMINIST BIBLICAL INTERPRETERS: THE QUILT'S FOUNDATION

For Elisabeth Schüssler Fiorenza, critical feminist biblical interpretation is more than a simple set of methods. Instead, she understands critical feminist biblical interpretation as a dynamic, fluid, and adaptable interaction between many elements. Most important among those elements are the humans who in the past, in the present, and in the future have influenced, do influence, or will be influenced by the biblical text and its interpretation.

Central to her interpretational theory, then, is the critical feminist biblical interpreter. Such a person does not aim simply to come to more "scientifically accurate" interpretations of the biblical texts. Instead, this person cultivates the ability to understand the kyriocentric context from which the biblical texts emerged. At the same time, the critical feminist biblical interpreter strives to untangle and expose the kyriarchal structures of domination that create oppressive interpretations of those texts. The critical feminist biblical interpreter sets as central to the interpretational method the status of women, their well-being or oppression in light of biblical interpretation, and how this contributes to both.

For Schüssler Fiorenza, feminist biblical interpretation means more than just discussing women in a biblical context. She stresses the importance of *critical* feminism as a core component of critical feminist biblical interpretation. The quilt square of critical feminism is made up of distinct, yet interlocking elements. First, Schüssler Fiorenza insists that critical feminism should not, especially when conceiving the meaning of gender, fall prey to the trap of essentialism. Gender is only one of many factors such as age, race, educational level, nationality, and sexual orientation, which can cause someone to be oppressed by kyriarchal structures. Second, Schüssler Fiorenza points out that a critical feminist continually examines not only the extent and nature of how she or he is oppressed by kyriarchy, but also how she or he might be participating in the perpetuation of that oppression. Third, the critical feminist engages in an assessment of the kyriocentrism within society by using critical thinking skills. This person becomes more and more conscious of both the overt and hidden ways in which people are dominated by elite men. In doing so, the critical feminist becomes more and more able to see how the Bible, its interpretation, and the methods used to interpret it all contribute to upholding the complex web of kyriarchal power structures that dominate women. The critical feminist biblical interpreter is a critical thinker who becomes continually more aware of kyriocentrism, how it harms, and how the biblical studies contribute to it.

Therefore, the critical feminist biblical interpreter sees the well-being or oppression of women, within the texts themselves or within the interpretation of texts, as a central concern of biblical interpretation. This does not mean, however, that more traditional methods or tools of interpretation are flatly rejected. Nevertheless, they are used with suspicion. The critical feminist biblical interpreter recalls that not only are the biblical texts themselves imbued with kyriocentric ideology, but that the very tools used to write and teach about those texts generally reflect the interests of people who wish to perpetuate kyriarchal power structures. While the feminist interpreter might use biblical dictionaries, encyclopedias, or academic papers, all of these tools will be viewed as "suspect" and capable of fostering kyriarchal interests. The critical feminist biblical interpreter studies and understands more traditional methods of biblical interpretation by taking from them what is useful and challenging in them what is harmful to women. To do this, however, one must have an acute awareness of his or her oppressive or oppressed situation.

Rather than begin with the assumption that the Bible is the normative, literal voice of God in written form, the critical feminist biblical interpreter sees her or his experience as equally important, if not more important, to the understanding and interpretation of biblical texts. Schüssler Fiorenza admits that this interpretational orientation has pitfalls, such as seeing experience as solely private. Nevertheless, by privileging the experience of women, and especially the experience of the woman who is a critical feminist biblical interpreter, Schüssler Fiorenza guards her theory of biblical interpretation from becoming a mere technique. Interpretational techniques are rarely able to adapt to the dynamic rhetorical situations the biblical interpreter often encounters. By creating an acute awareness of the role or position in society as both an oppressed and perhaps oppressing person, Schüssler Fiorenza's critical feminist biblical interpreter can apply techniques of interpretation tailored to a particular situation and experience. This enables the biblical interpreter to choose the interpretational technique best suited to uncover kyriarchal interests in the texts and/or in their interpretations.

Schüssler Fiorenza's theory of biblical interpretation, although it contains many suggested interpretational methods, centers its main efforts instead on developing a particular type of person: a critical feminist biblical interpreter. This person develops as a result of a transformational process. This person moves from viewing reality through the lens of kyriocentrism, often unconsciously, to perceiving reality in terms of liberation by viewing it through the lens of critical feminist biblical interpretation. Once this metamorphosis of perception begins, the critical feminist biblical interpreter starts becoming an agent of transformation and liberation for the benefit of all.

THE RHETORICAL-EMANCIPATORY CONTEXT: THE QUILT'S FRAME

In her book *Wisdom Ways: Introducing Feminist Biblical Interpretation*, Schüssler Fiorenza invites her readers to join her on a path that she and others helped to create. Her critical feminist hermeneutic of liberation began, perhaps, even as far back as her childhood as a refugee. Later, when she came to America, she found an academic atmosphere that, although not fully in sympathy with her ideas, allowed her to develop and evolve a whole new field of interpretive inquiry in biblical studies. Schüssler Fiorenza notes, "in the last twenty-five years feminist biblical studies have been established as a new area of inquiry with its own publications. It is taught in schools, colleges, and universities and is practiced by many scholars in different parts of the world."[99] Less than three decades ago, feminist biblical studies did not exist as a discipline. Today, the field is both unified and diverse, and Schüssler Fiorenza continues to play a major role in shaping its direction. She points to three major concepts with which most feminist biblical scholars agree:

1. The Bible is written in androcentric and kyriocentric language and serves patriarchal interests.

2. The Bible came into being in patriarchal societies, cultures, and religions.

3. The Bible is still proclaimed and taught today in patriarchal/kyriarchal societies and religions.[100]

The language and the interests of the Bible have always been and remain today focused on supporting structures of kyriarchal power. Indeed, some feminists reject the idea that the Bible can ever be used to foster a belief in equality and freedom for all, and therefore dismiss it. Schüssler Fiorenza agrees wholeheartedly with the three premises listed above, but she also reasons that because the Bible plays such a major role in the everyday lives of women, its interpretation cannot be ignored. In order to assist women in interpreting the Bible in a manner that will not harm, and might even help, Schüssler Fiorenza proposes that a fourth concept could be added to the three listed above.

4. In and through a critical interpretive process, the Bible can function as a spiritual vision and a resource in struggles for freedom and liberation.[101]

Schüssler Fiorenza's critical interpretive process is more than just a method; it is a transformation of a person's perceptions. It includes not only an investigation of biblical texts, but also an investigation of the social, cultural, religious, and economic contexts of the texts themselves, the people in the texts, the people who wrote the texts, the people who use the texts—past and present—as documents of authority, and those who read the texts and derive meaning for their lives. More than this,

Schüssler Fiorenza insists that those interpretations that tend to harm women should be viewed with deep suspicion and most likely rejected. The rejection of these interpretations should come not from the fact that they do not adhere to a particular methodology, but from the fact that they do not advance the struggles of women for liberation.

Thus the rhetorical context of biblical studies in Schüssler Fiorenza's view must be seen in terms of the well-being or harm of women. To some, this sounds too ideological. Consider, however, the fact that all interpretational methods are ideological. Schüssler Fiorenza states her method in a forthright, honest fashion and does not hide behind the mask of supposed objectivity. She chooses to be a critical feminist biblical interpreter because, for her, it is an ethical choice. Now we will turn our attention to how one actually becomes a critical feminist biblical interpreter.

PIECES OF SCHÜSSLER FIORENZA'S INTERPRETATIONAL THEORY

Although Elisabeth Schüssler Fiorenza, throughout her many writings, offers suggestions for transforming oneself into a critical feminist biblical interpreter, the following sentence provides an apt summary. It includes many of the quilt squares Schüssler Fiorenza uses to explain her idea of what it means to be a critical feminist biblical interpreter: " . . . becoming a feminist interpreter means shifting your focus from biblical interpretation construed as an ever better explanation of the text to biblical interpretation as a tool for becoming conscious of structures of domination and for articulating visions of a radical democracy that are inscribed in our own experience as well as in that of the texts." [102]

This sentence exemplifies Elisabeth Schüssler Fiorenza's view of what it means to be a critical feminist biblical interpreter. One can both explicitly and implicitly find in it much of Schüssler Fiorenza's critical feminist method of interpretation, and, more importantly, the transformation that must occur in order to create a critical feminist biblical interpreter. We will look at the sentence, word by word, to discover the hidden depths and varieties of meaning Schüssler Fiorenza has woven into its fabric. When we are finished, we will see that the sentence is, much like Schüssler Fiorenza's work as a whole, a tapestry or quilt sewn together from carefully chosen ideas, concepts, critiques, observations, and methodologies.

Because Schüssler Fiorenza's critical feminist hermeneutic of liberation resists the linear, assembly-line practices of other methods, it seems appropriate to see the interconnected whole of her interpretational method in this intricately interwoven sentence. Schüssler Fiorenza sees biblical interpretation as a rhetorical-emancipatory project that provides a multifaceted lens to use as a tool for biblical interpretation. Her methodology is not meant to provide a way to interpret a text "correctly" once and for all, even from a feminist perspective. Instead, she seeks to create interpreters who are able to interpret and discern biblical texts within many complex contexts to see whether they tend to liberate or oppress. Remember, the same biblical text might function to help in one context, but might prove harmful in another. "Who is trying to persuade whom of what and for what reason?" might be a core question to use in order to practice Schüssler Fiorenza's critical feminist hermeneutic of liberation. With this in mind, we turn to Schüssler Fiorenza's explanation of what it means to become a feminist interpreter.

Schüssler Fiorenza's use of the word "becoming" is important. It implies that her theory of biblical interpretation does not rely solely on a set of methods, but relies instead on transformed people who become critical feminist biblical interpreters. The word also suggests an important element of Schüssler Fiorenza's theory: movement. Schüssler Fiorenza uses movement as a central metaphor to explain her theory. Of course, people generally prefer metaphors that support and uphold kyriocentrism to describe biblical interpretation. In fact, kyriocentric biblical interpreters often erroneously liken their efforts to those of research scientists. Schüssler Fiorenza notes that other theorists of feminist interpretation use metaphors of movement such as "making visible," "hearing into speech," and "finding one's voice"[103] to communicate what they mean by feminist biblical interpretation. Schüssler Fiorenza appreciates and even employs these metaphors, but she specifically imagines critical feminist biblical interpretation using the metaphor of dance, whether it is the dance of light on ocean waves or the dance of a person expressing him or herself in nonlinear, creative, and imaginative ways. Becoming a critical feminist biblical interpreter means learning and practicing various "moves" or "dance steps."[104]

In this dance, one who is becoming a critical feminist biblical interpreter learns to dance between two extremes: the pseudo-objectivity of those who see interpretation of the Bible as a scientific venture, and the relativistic extreme of those who see interpretation as a "free-for-all" wherein nothing can be known.[105] By dancing between these two extremes, a transformation begins to occur. A critical feminist biblical interpreter learns many dance steps and develops the ability to move from one rhetorical context to another in order to explore and to understand the many ways a biblical text functions within a variety of situations.

This ability to negotiate the path between objectivity and relativism does not develop overnight. Often the kyriocentric culture within which a person has grown up and lived has such a powerful influence that she or he might see kyriarchal and androcentric ideas as simply common sense or the way things were meant to be. Schüssler Fiorenza points to several roadblocks one might encounter when becoming a critical feminist biblical interpreter.

BEING A FEMINIST

Feminism, beyond any other term that Schüssler Fiorenza uses, evokes criticism from both academia and the public at large. Both generally label Schüssler Fiorenza's theory of biblical interpretation as ideological and biased. We must remember, however, that even so-called "objective" or "scientific" methods of biblical interpretation were developed by, and are practiced by humans—all of whom have their own ideologies and biases. Schüssler Fiorenza informs her readers of her ideological stance in an honest, straightforward manner. Instead of supporting the preservation of kyriocentrism and the elite men it generally favors, Schüssler Fiorenza fosters the well-being of women who have been oppressed, erased, and often harmed by the pseudo-objectivity of traditional biblical interpretation. Since biblical interpretation involves more than set pieces of method, Schüssler Fiorenza hopes humans will be transformed and become feminist biblical interpreters, or, more accurately, critical feminist biblical interpreters.

For Schüssler Fiorenza, one's method of interpretation either upholds kyriarchal structures of oppression or works against them. For Schüssler Fiorenza, feminism, "the radical notion that wo/men are people too" provides a position of identification with the oppressed, rather than against them.[106] To this end, she argues that feminist interpreters, and all interpreters, must not only interpret the texts and their surrounding social/historical contexts, they must also analyze their own social/ideological position. Feminism is one of the few ideological stances that actually performs this self-criticism in the open. Other, more traditional ideologies just assume they make common sense because they are already inscribed in culture by virtue of privilege.

THE INTERPRETER

Schüssler Fiorenza's use of the word *interpreter* implies something many people rarely consider. If one listens to a discussion about the Bible, or hears a preacher give a sermon, one will often hear the phrase, "The Bible says. . . . ." But as we have seen, the Bible does not actually speak. Instead, humans read the Bible and then interpret what they have read. Everyone who reads the Bible interprets it, whether they are conscious of doing so or not. For some people, the phrase "the Bible says . . ." might only be used as a convenience. But for many more, it is a phrase that is often used to justify a personal opinion and back it up with what seems to be a solid dictate from the Bible. Often, this personal opinion, as Schüssler Fiorenza points out, is a justification of kyriarchal power structures.

The phrase "the Bible says. . . " really should be phrased, "I interpret the Bible to mean. . . ." Claiming the Bible says something is itself an interpretation. Ironically, the more one insists that she or he is not interpreting the Bible, the more one is actually insisting upon a specific interpretation of it. We cannot escape the process of interpretation. We do it either consciously or unconsciously. Schüssler Fiorenza, of course, goes further, arguing that the way we interpret either upholds or resists kyriarchy. We cannot choose whether or not to be an interpreter, but we can, and should, Schüssler Fiorenza argues, choose what kind of interpreter we become. For her, that choice is not simply methodological, but also ethical.

BECOMING A FEMINIST INTERPRETER

We might summarize Schüssler Fiorenza's ideal for a critical feminist biblical interpreter in one word: *awareness.* For Schüssler Fiorenza, awareness is a process. During this process, a person becomes more and more conscious of feminist concerns, such as the problems caused by kyriocentrism and the need to fight for the well-being of all women. To this end, Schüssler Fiorenza hopes that as people become increasingly aware of these ideas, they will become ethically conscious interpreters. For Schüssler Fiorenza, this means transformation from seeing the assumptions of kyriocentrism as normal to seeing them as harmful, and then seeking a solution.

THE POWER TO NAME

Throughout most of history women have had to struggle to have any voice at all in the production of meaning and the defining of ideas. The issue is often seen as the question of the *power to name.* Those who have the power generally name the rules by which ideas, principles, and even moral values of a society are defined and evaluated. Remember that much of traditional biblical interpretation prefers to name itself as "objective" and "value-neutral," evaluating itself as trustworthy and reliable, even though it is quite often blatantly kyriocentric.

However, traditional biblical interpretation, because it has at the moment the power to name, labels feminist biblical interpretation as biased and ideological. Thanks to scholars such as Schüssler Fiorenza, women are more frequently challenging such definitions. We have seen that purely value-neutral interpretations are not possible; hence, the labeling of feminist interpretation as ideological falls short of the objectivity it claims. Most people do not understand this, nor have they really thought carefully about it. The ability and power to name, therefore, is for Schüssler Fiorenza a key characteristic of the critical feminist biblical interpreter.

SHIFTING YOUR FOCUS

People do not like to shift their focus. Schüssler Fiorenza frequently notes that the shift from seeing the world through the eyes of kyriocentrism, which is seen as normal, to seeing the

FEMINISM

Elisabeth Schüssler Fiorenza defines feminism in one sentence that could easily be placed on a bumper sticker: "Feminism is the radical notion that wo/men are people." It seems simple enough, but when one contemplates it, several layers of meaning emerge. First, feminism is a radical notion. Schüssler Fiorenza almost always notes that the word radical goes back to the Latin word *radix*, meaning root. Thus, feminism is a root, or central notion, not a novel idea from the fringes of philosophy, religious theory, or theology. It is a core human value that seeks the well-being of all people. Second, feminism argues that women are people of value. Most often, women are defined by their oppressors. They have been labeled as slaves, wives, servants, welfare queens, migrant workers, and refugees. At the root, however, feminism argues that, instead of seeing women only in terms of their kyriocentrically defined roles, we should see them as humans of worth. Third, once we see women as human beings, their oppressive status within kyriarchal society will become apparent. Instead of seeing women as natural servants, we will see them as exploited humans, and, Schüssler Fiorenza hopes, will be moved to do something about it.

world through the eyes of liberation and feminism, which is seen as abnormal, can be an uncomfortable and disturbing process. People like that which is familiar. They will often choose that which is familiar over that which is not, even if the familiar harms them in some way. Schüssler Fiorenza points out that women themselves will often resist the shift from kyriarchal structures of domination to liberation. This is because women have come to identify with the kyriocentrism they have been taught to see as normal.

Further, the shift which Schüssler Fiorenza argues the critical feminist biblical interpreter must undergo is a full shift in focus. It is a personal, individual process that Schüssler Fiorenza imagines. It belongs to the individual interpreter, not to any outside authority that insists on one dominant theory or method. The critical feminist biblical interpreter relies on individual experiences and personal views of the world, and then interweaves them with the tools of biblical interpretation that work best.

Shifting your focus involves a reorientation of the mind and the heart. Most people have been culturally conditioned to accept kyriocentric ideas, without even thinking about where they come from or how they help or hurt. The shift about which Schüssler Fiorenza speaks is a shift that begins the process of liberating women to resist kyriarchy.

AN EVER BETTER EXPLANATION OF THE TEXT
Schüssler Fiorenza suggests that a critical feminist biblical interpreter should avoid the assumptions of the more traditional models of interpreting the Bible. In doing so she rejects both the Doctrinal-Revelatory Paradigm and the Scientific-Positivist Paradigm. Both paradigms assume that the closer one comes to the "best" meaning of the text, the more authority one's interpretation has. We have seen, however, that this notion is flawed for at least two reasons. First, interpreters can never rid themselves completely of bias or ideology. Therefore, all interpretations necessarily include an ideological angle. Second, biblical texts are tainted with kyriocentric ideology and androcentric language.

Biblical interpretation seen simply a matter of finding "an ever better explanation of the text" assumes that the text itself is a standard, possessing both normative and authoritative qualities. But since the biblical texts themselves uphold kyriarchal power structures, the ability to come closer and closer to their meaning actually upholds the oppression of women.

A TOOL FOR BECOMING CONSCIOUS
OF STRUCTURES OF DOMINATION

Because the Bible was produced in social and historical contexts of kyriocentrism and written in the language of androcentrism, some feminist scholars dismiss it altogether. Although Schüssler Fiorenza understands their point of view, she sees the Bible and its interpretation as vital to the well-being of women. She therefore attempts to develop interpreters who can use the interpretation of the Bible not simply as a source of what is normative or authoritative, but as a "tool" to help women better understand just how they are oppressed by kyriarchal power structures.

How biblical interpretation functions, however, depends upon how it is "construed." If it is construed in the traditional way, then it will most likely perpetuate the structures of domination that harm women. If, however, as Schüssler Fiorenza suggests, it is construed as a tool to make women aware of kyriarchy, then biblical interpretation can actually help women. A key component of resisting kyriarchal domination is first to be aware of its existence and its structures. Schüssler Fiorenza applauds biblical interpretation that stimulates that awareness.

ARTICULATING VISIONS OF RADICAL DEMOCRACY

Schüssler Fiorenza's theory of biblical interpretation does much more than interrupt, tear down, and resist kyriocentric interpretations of the Bible that harm women. Schüssler Fiorenza's theory attempts to produce critical feminist biblical interpreters who can develop an alternative model to the kyriocentric society.

Again, we learn much by looking deeply into the implications of some of these specific words:

Articulating

One of the problems confronting feminist interpreters is that so many women's voices throughout history, and even today, have been silenced. Indeed, Schüssler Fiorenza points out that this trend so pervades the stereotypical conception about women, that women themselves often feel self-conscious when they do speak out. This culturally conditioned hesitancy, Schüssler Fiorenza contends, must be overcome. Since critical feminism begins with personal experience, the ability to articulate that personal experience is one of the keys to becoming a critical feminist biblical interpreter. More than this, the critical feminist must develop the ability to communicate the personal and individual toll kyriarchal structures inflict upon her or him. Then, having exposed the destructive nature of kyriocentrism, the critical feminist biblical interpreter must form an alternative idea, a "vision."

Visions

Schüssler Fiorenza is not naive about completely transforming the kyriocentrism of society overnight. She nevertheless includes in her theory elements of hope and possibility. For her, imagination is key. She believes that it is important to develop the ability to articulate visions of those possibilities. Perhaps to point out that no one person's vision should dominate, Schüssler Fiorenza refers to "visions" in the plural. As we shall see, Schüssler Fiorenza's ideal of a "radical democracy" hopes to foster multiple, dynamic, interacting visions of women's well-being.

Radical Democracy

The critical feminist biblical interpreter critiques and exposes the oppressive nature or kyriarchy. However, she or he also provides an alternative—radical democracy—usually, in Schüssler Fiorenza's writings, accompanied by the concept of "ekklēsia of wo/men." The "ekklēsia of wo/men," is a term Schüssler Fiorenza uses as a counterbalance to the elite male-dominated traditional church. It means both democratic society and democratic church. The term seeks to overcome the split between secular and religious women's movements. By specifically naming the role of women within the "church" assembly or gathering, that is, ekklēsia, she redefines what it means to "do church." In Schüssler Fiorenza's vision, the church is actually an ekklēsia, a group of people gathered together for a common struggle. She names this group the "ekklēsia of wo/men" to intentionally include those who have traditionally been left out of the power structures of the church.

Within the ekklēsia of wo/men, then, radical democracy is the preferred system of operation. Radical democracy stands in direct opposition to the principles of kyriarchy, upon which the governmental system of the traditional church is built. Schüssler Fiorenza chooses to use the word "radical" because it comes from the Latin word *radix,* meaning root. She bases her notion of radical democracy not only on modern democratic theory, but also on a reconstruction of the early Jesus movement recovered in her works from practicing a critical hermeneutics of suspicion and liberation upon the New Testament texts. Before the early church adapted its power structures to match those of the Roman Empire, it had within it elements and pockets of radical democracy. It attracted women and even promoted many of them to positions of power. Although Schüssler Fiorenza does not see this an ideal time for women, she nevertheless points out that the Jesus movement did indeed manifest characteristics of radical democracy. She seeks to reach back to its roots and recover its core values for use today.

If we compare kyriarchal churches to the radical democracy of Schüssler Fiorenza's ekklēsia of wo/men, we will see sharp contrasts. Kyriarchal churches employ a hierarchal system of power based in varying degrees upon the ancient system of power within the Roman Empire. The ekklēsia of wo/men, meanwhile, strives to foster egalitarianism. It sees each woman as able and capable of leadership within the group. This does not mean, however, that the ekklēsia of wo/men strives for sameness in all its members. Unlike kyriarchal churches that often insist on uniformity of belief and behavior among their members, the ekklēsia of wo/men honors the differences various women bring. Within a radical democracy, a multiplicity of voices strengthens the whole rather than diminishing it. Equality, therefore, in Schüssler Fiorenza's ekklēsia of wo/men does not mean sameness.

While kyriarchal churches often appoint men to lifetime positions of power, the ekklēsia of wo/men prefers alternating leadership. This prevents the temptation to use one's power to create and uphold structures within the church that perpetuate one's own powerful and privileged position. In the ekklēsia of wo/men all women would eventually lead. Thus, rather than having one's spiritual life dictated from above by a hierarchy, in the ekklēsia of wo/men the value of self-determination is cherished. Decisions about who rules come up from the group, not down from a hierarchy.

Often, kyriarchal churches can seem to be rather exclusive in their assessment of who can and who cannot be a member of, or participate in, the church. In contrast, the ekklēsia of wo/men sees inclusiveness as a core value. Most often, kyriarchal churches exclude various groups of women from church or church leadership on the bases of what they deem to be a biblical mandate. As we have seen, however, much of the traditional church's interpretation of the scripture biases itself toward the perpetuation of kyriocentric values, and thus should be viewed with suspicion. Because the ekklēsia of wo/men uses as its interpretational method the critical feminist hermeneutics of liberation, it invites those people other churches often excluded. It also has no difficulty encouraging women to fully participate by taking up alternating roles of leadership and authority. This will only server to foster an even more inclusive ekklēsia.

The ekklēsia of wo/men uses the principles of radical democracy to promote and to privilege the well-being of women. In contrast to kyriarchal churches that often see the continuation of the authority structure as key, the ekklēsia of wo/men shifts its focus to liberating women. It provides a space for getting together, for sharing ideas, for debating issues, and for many other activities depending upon what the women of the ekklēsia need at the moment. Rather than viewing the church as something to be served by women, the ekklēsia of wo/men sees itself and its women in a dynamic, symbiotic relationship—helping each other from positions of equality and respect.

The critical feminist biblical interpreter, therefore, has a daunting task. To articulate the visions of the ekklēsia of

THE QUESTION OF FEMALE ORDINATION

One of the core issues facing modern Christianity is whether or not to ordain females as priests or pastors. Some Christian denominations, such as the United Methodists, the American Baptists, the Evangelical Lutheran Church in America, and the Episcopal Church, already do. Other large churches do not ordain females, notably the Catholic Church and the Southern Baptist Convention, the largest Protestant denomination in the United States. One might assume that as a feminist biblical interpreter, Schüssler Fiorenza wishes that as many females as possible would be ordained as soon as possible, but this would be oversimplifying her position on the subject.

For Schüssler Fiorenza, the cost of a female becoming a priest or pastor may be too high. This cost often involves blending in to the kyriarchal structures of an existing church and educational system. She notes that while some churches will ordain females, most will resist ordaining a critical feminist female concerned with the liberation and well-being of women. Thus, Schüssler Fiorenza warns females that in order to obtain ordination, they might have to abandon or suppress their liberationist ideas. At various places in her career, Schüssler Fiorenza expresses the view that this might be too profound a sacrifice. On the other hand, Schüssler Fiorenza seems to encourage females who can qualify for ordination while maintaining their feminist, liberationist ideals. The issue then, is not simply to infuse the church with more female priests or pastors, but to encourage females to change the church while remaining true to critical feminist ideals of liberation.

wo/men and radical democracy, the critical feminist must look both within and to the biblical texts. To do this, she or he must undergo a shift in focus from kyriocentric methods of biblical interpretation to seeing the world through the critical feminist hermeneutic of liberation. It is a choice, a transformation, and a worldview. It is not, as Schüssler Fiorenza frequently points out, a one-size-fits-all method. The critical feminist biblical interpreter must at all times understand the rhetorical situation she or he is presently in, the rhetorical situation that produced the biblical text, and the rhetorical situation that produced the kyriarchal interpretations of the text. In all of this, the critical feminist biblical interpreter chooses the well-being of women and the resistance of kyriarchy as the central lens through which to view the world. This is a choice not of convenience or wishful thinking, but of ethics and humanity. Schüssler Fiorenza's groundbreaking method of biblical interpretation, therefore, requires the contributions of people who are willing to choose an ethical, human, interpretational framework that helps women. For Elisabeth Schüssler Fiorenza, this is a life goal. She has in the past and continues today to demonstrate a devotion to this cause through her work and her life.

1938   Elisabeth Schüssler Fiorenza is born.

1939-1945   World War II is fought on several fronts.

1945-1946   Elisabeth and her family move to Germany.

1958   Elisabeth graduates from Humanistisches Gymnasium (prep school) in Germany.

1962   Elisabeth earns her theologicum (the equivalent of her master of divinity degree); she is the first woman in her university to study the full course of theology usually only taken by seminarians to be ordained.

1938
Birth of Elisabeth Schüssler Fiorenza

1970
Schüssler Fiorenza graduates from the University of Münster in Germany with a doctorate in theology

1935   1950   1970

1958
Elisabeth graduates from Humanistisches Gymnasium (prep school) in Germany

1963
Elisabeth earns her licentiate degree in pastoral theology

1962
Elisabeth earns her master of divinity degree

1964   Schüssler Fiorenza's first book in German is published.

1970   Schüssler Fiorenza graduates from the University of Münster in Germany with a doctorate in theology.

1970–1984   Schüssler Fiorenza teaches theology at the University of Notre Dame.

1972   Schüssler Fiorenza's dissertation is published in German.

1983   Schüssler Fiorenza publishes *In Memory of Her.*

1983
Schüssler Fiorenza publishes
In Memory of Her

1985
Schüssler Fiorenza and Judith Plaskow start
the *Journal of Feminist Studies in Religion*

1980   1990   2001

1994
The tenth anniversary edition
of *In Memory of Her* is released

2001
Schüssler Fiorenza
publishes *Wisdom Ways*

CHRONOLOGY

1984   Schüssler Fiorenza publishes *Bread Not Stone: The Challenge of Feminist Biblical Interpretation.*

1984–1988   Schüssler Fiorenza teaches at the Episcopal Divinity School in Cambridge, Massachusetts.

1985–present   Schüssler Fiorenza is cofounder of the *Journal of Feminist Studies in Religion.*

1987   Schüssler Fiorenza delivers a significant address as president of the Society of Biblical Literature.

1988–present   Schüssler Fiorenza is a Krister Stendahl professor at the Divinity School of Harvard University.

1991   Schüssler Fiorenza publishes *Revelation: Vision of a Just World.*

1992   Schüssler Fiorenza publishes *But She Said: Feminist Practices of Biblical Interpretation.*

1993   Schüssler Fiorenza publishes *Discipleship of Equals: A Critical Feminist ekklēsia-logy of liberation* and *Searching the Scriptures: A Feminist Introduction.*

1994   Schüssler Fiorenza publishes *Jesus: Miriam's Child, Sophia's Prophet: Critical Issues in Feminist Christology;* the tenth anniversary edition of *In Memory of Her* is released.

1995–present   Schüssler Fiorenza is co-chair of Feminist Liberation Theologians Network.

1999   Schüssler Fiorenza publishes *Rhetoric and Ethic: The Politics of Biblical Studies.*

2001   Schüssler Fiorenza publishes *Wisdom Ways.*

NOTES

CHAPTER 1:
A Childhood Lesson Learned

1. Fernando F. Segovia, ed., *Toward a New Heaven and a New Earth: Essays in Honor of Elisabeth Schüssler Fiorenza,* "Looking Back, Looking Around, Looking Ahead: An Interview with Elisabeth Schüssler Fiorenza" (Maryknoll, N.Y.: Orbis Books, 2003), p. 26.

2. Elisabeth Schüssler Fiorenza, *Wisdom Ways: Introducing Feminist Biblical Interpretation* (Maryknoll, N.Y.: Orbis Books, 2001), p. 3.

3. Ibid., p. 9.

CHAPTER 2:
From Refugee To Pioneer

4. Elisabeth Schüssler Fiorenza, "Wartime as Formative," *The Christian Century* (August 16–23 ,1995), pp. 778–779.

5. Fernando F. Segovia, ed., *Toward a New Heaven and a New Earth: Essays in Honor of Elisabeth Schüssler Fiorenza,* "Looking Back, Looking Around, Looking Ahead: An Interview with Elisabeth Schüssler Fiorenza" (Maryknoll, N.Y.: Orbis Books, 2003), p. 4.

6. Schüssler Fiorenza, "Wartime as Formative," p. 1.

7. Ibid., pp. 1–2.

8. Segovia, p. 2.

9. Ibid., p. 4.

10. Segovia, p. 5.

11. Annie Lally Millhaven, ed., *The Inside Stories: 13 Valiant Women Challenging the Church* (Mystic, Conn.: Twenty-Third Publications, 1987), p. 51.

12. Ibid., p. 44.

13. Ibid.

14. Ibid.

15. Segovia, p. 7.

16. Ibid.

17. Ibid.

18. Ibid.

19. Ibid., p. 8.

20. Segovia, p. 13.

21. Ibid., p. 14.

22. Ibid.

23. Millhaven, p. 51.

24. Segovia, p. 13.

25. Ibid.

26. Ibid.

27. Ibid.

28. Elisabeth Schüssler Fiorenza, *In Memory of Her: A Feminist Theological Reconstruction of Christian Origins* (New York: Crossroads Publishers, 1994).

29. Millhaven, p. 55.

30. Ibid.

31. Ibid.

32. Millhaven, pp. 61–62.

33. Ibid., p. 60.

34. Ibid.

35. Elisabeth Schüssler Fiorenza, Interview with Maria Bucciarelli, Society of Biblical Literature forum, 2003 (www.sbl-site.org/Article.aspx?ArticleId=68).

36. Ibid.

37. Ibid.

38. Segovia, p. 22.

39. Ibid., p. 26.

40. Ibid.

CHAPTER 3: The Challenge of *In Memory of Her*

41. Elisabeth Schüssler Fiorenza, *In Memory of Her: A Feminist Theological Reconstruction of Christian Origins* (New York: Crossroads Publishers, 1994), pp. xiiv, xiv.

42. Ibid., p. 92.

43. Ibid.

44. Elisabeth Schüssler Fiorenza, *Jesus and the Politics of interpretation* (New York: Continuum International Publishing Group, 2000), pp. 123–124.

45. Schüssler Fiorenza, *In Memory of Her,* p. xiv.

46. Ibid.

47. Ibid.

48. Ibid., p. xv.

49. Ibid.

50. Schüssler Fiorenza, *In Memory of Her.* p. xv.
51. Ibid.
52. Ibid., p. xvi.
53. Ibid., pp. xvi–xvii.
54. Ibid., p. xvii.
55. Ibid.
56. Ibid, p. xvi.
57. Ibid., p. xvii.
58. Ibid., p. xx.
59. Ibid., p. xvii.
60. Ibid., p. xxii.
61. Ibid.
62. Ibid., p. xxiv.
63. Ibid., p. xxv.
64. Ibid., p. xxvi.
65. Ibid.
66. Ibid.
67. Ibid., p. xxix.
68. Ibid., p. xxx.
69. Ibid.
70. Ibid., p. xxxii
71. Ibid., p. xxxv.
72. Ibid.
73. Ibid., p. xxxi.
74. Ibid., p. xxxiv.
75. Ibid.
76. Ibid., p. xxxv.
77. Ibid.
78. Ibid.

CHAPTER 4: A Variety of Biblical Interpretations

79. Elisabeth Schüssler Fiorenza, *Wisdom Ways: Introducing Feminist Biblical Interpretation* (Maryknoll, N.Y.: Orbis Books, 2001), p. 40.
80. Ibid.
81. Ibid., p. 39.
82. Ibid., p. 40.
83. Ibid., p. 51.
84. Ibid., p. 41.
85. Ibid.
86. Ibid., pp. 41–42.
87. Ibid., p. 42.
88. Ibid.
89. Ibid.
90. Ibid.
91. Ibid., p. 52.
92. Ibid., p. 43.
93. Ibid.
94. Ibid., p. 44.
95. Ibid.
96. Ibid., p. 52.
97. Ibid.
98. Ibid., p. 45.

CHAPTER 5:
A Quilt of Many Colors

99. Elisabeth Schüssler Fiorenza, *Wisdom Ways: Introducing Feminist Biblical Interpretation* (Maryknoll, N.Y.: Orbis Books, 2001), p. 9.
100. Ibid.
101. Ibid.
102. Ibid.
103. Ibid., p. 166.
104. Ibid.
105. Ibid., p. 168.
106. Ibid.

androcentric—Dominated by or emphasizing male interests or a male point of view.

anti-Semitism—Hostility toward or discrimination against Jews.

basileia—A term that refers to an empire.

conscientization—The process of consciousness raising that allows women to understand and name the processes and structures of their oppression and the structures of privilege.

critical feminist biblical interpreter—Someone who can understand the structures of kyriarchy inherent both in the discipline of interpreting biblical texts and within the biblical texts themselves.

ekklēsia—A democratic assembly.

empiricism—Relying on observation and experiment.

Enlightenment—An intellectual movement in Europe in the 1900s.

essentialism—A philosophical theory that "essentializes" or assigns importance to only one particular part of a whole.

exegesis—Historical criticism.

fellowship—A grant or position.

feminism—A concept that raises the consciousness of both females and males and helps them understand the oppressive structures that entangle them.

Franciscans—An order of monks devoted to preaching, missions, and charity.

gymnasium—The German version of college preparatory classes or prep schools in America.

hermeneutics—The study of the methodological principles of interpretation (in this case of the Bible).

kyriarchy—A complex pattern of societal domination by elite males over those people who are not privileged.

licentiate—An academic degree ranking below that of a doctor given by some European universities.

Mardi Gras—A carnival period often observed with festivals and parades that culminates on the day before Ash Wednesday.

metaphor—A figure of speech in which a word or phrase literally denoting one idea is used in place of another to suggest a likeness between them.

paradigm—An outstanding clear or typical example or pattern.

PaRDeS–An acronym for a method of biblical interpretation in Judaism.

refugee—A person who flees to a foreign country to escape danger or persecution.

summa cum laude—With highest distinction.

tenure—A status granted after a trial period to a teacher that gives protection from unwarranted dismissal.

theology—The study of God.

Wisdom-Sophia—An alternative way of thinking about and personifying the divine.

wo/men—The term Elisabeth Schüssler Fiorenza uses to refer to both women and men who experience oppression in any form.

Milhaven Annie Lally, ed. *The Inside Stories: 13 Valiant Women Challenging the Church.* Mystic, Conn.: Twenty-Third Publications, 1987.

Schüssler Fiorenza, Elisabeth. *In Memory of Her: A Feminist Theological Reconstruction of Christian Origins. Tenth Anniversary Edition.* New York: Crossroad Publishers, 1994.

Schüssler Fiorenza, Elisabeth. Interview with Maria Bucciarelli, Society of Biblical Literature forum, 2003 (www.sbl-site.org/Article.aspx?ArticleId=68).

Schüssler Fiorenza, Elisabeth. *Jesus and the Politics of Interpretation.* New York: Continuum, 2000.

Schüssler Fiorenza, Elisabeth. "Wartime as Formative," *The Christian Century.* Vol. 112, issue 24. August 16 1995.

Schüssler Fiorenza, Elisabeth. *Wisdom Ways: Introducing Feminist Biblical Interpretation.* New York: Orbis Books, 2001.

Segovia, Fernando, ed. *Toward a New Heaven and a New Earth: Essays in Honor of Elisabeth Schüssler Fiorenza.* "Looking Back, Looking Around, Looking Ahead: An Interview with Elisabeth Schüssler Fiorenza." New York: Orbis Books, 2003.

FURTHER READING

PRIMARY SOURCES

Agosin, Marjorie. *Women, Gender, and Human Rights: A Global Perspective.* New Brunswick, N.J.: Rutgers University Press, 2001.

Bristow, John T. *What Paul Really Said About Women: The Apostle's Liberating Views on Equality in Marriage, Leadership, and Love.* San Francisco: Harper, 1991.

Castelli, Elizabeth and Rosamond C. Rodman, eds. *Women, Gender, Religion: A Reader.* New York: Macmillan, 2001.

Clouse, Bonidell and Robert G. Clouse. *Women in Ministry: Four Views.* Downers Grove, Il.: InterVarsity Press, 1989.

Grenz, Stanley J. and Denise Muir Kjesbo. *Women in the Church: A Biblical Theology of Women in Ministry.* Downers Grove, Il.: InterVarsity Press, 1995.

Mass, Wendy. *Women's Rights.* San Diego, Calif.: Lucent Books, 1998.

WEBSITES

Elisabeth Schüssler Fiorenza's Theories
http://www.theology.ie/theologians/schuessler.htm
Useful summaries of her work and the work of others in her field.

Women Priests
http://www.womenpriests.org/classic/wp_cont.htm
Numerous full-text articles, including one on the twelve disciples by Elisabeth Schüssler Fiorenza.

Wabash Center: Guide to Internet Resources for Teaching and Learning in Theology and Religion
http://www.wabashcenter.wabash.edu/Internet/bible_new.htm
Historical ideas surrounding the issues of New Testament formation and Biblical Studies at the academic level.

Journal of Feminist Studies in Religion
http://www.hds.harvard.edu/jfsr/
Home page of the Journal of Feminist Studies in Religion, cofounded by Elisabeth Schüssler Fiorenza and Judith Plaskow.

Womanist Theory and Research

http://www.uga.edu/~womanist/

A solid resource with useful links for learning about Womanist theory.

Minnesota Advocates for Human Rights: "Fleeing for Your Life"
Refugee Role Play

http://mahr.extranet.urbanplanet.com/_Fleeing_for_Your_Life__-_Refugee_Role_Play.html

An excellent site to give students a feel for the life of a refugee.

INDEX

All images are courtesy of Dr. Elisabeth Schüssler Fiorenza.

ABOUT THE CONTRIBUTORS

GLEN ENANDER is Professor of Religion at South Dakota State University where he teaches Introduction to Religion, World Religions, Old and New Testament, and Native American Religion. He holds Masters of Arts degrees in both Theology and English. He has delivered conference papers on rhetoric, pedagogy, and the interaction between literature and religion. His research interests center on the formational process of religious myth/belief and how this process influences the lives and perceptions of various groups. He lives with two large dogs that continually teach him that food is good, and walks are better.

MARTIN E. MARTY is an ordained minister in the Evangelical Lutheran Church and the Fairfax M. Cone Distinguished Service Professor Emeritus at the University of Chicago Divinity School, where he taught for thirty-five years. Marty has served as president of the American Academy of Religion, the American Society of Church History, and the American Catholic Historical Association, and was also a member of two U.S. presidential commissions. He is currently Senior Regent at St. Olaf College in Northfield, Minnesota. Marty has written more than fifty books, including the three-volume *Modern American Religion* (University of Chicago Press). His book *Righteous Empire* was a recipient of the National Book Award.